Incident over Mostar

The story of the crew of the B-24H Heavy Bomber *Boojum*

By David F. Abner

ISBN: 1-59571-012-4
Library of Congress Control Number: 2004106259

Foreword and Acknowledgements

On April 27, 1992, my father, Frederick G. Abner Jr., passed away due to complications following cancer surgery. Because he was a World War II veteran and former German prisoner of war, and because he had lived in close proximity to Arlington, Virginia, our family arranged for his funeral to be held at Arlington National Cemetery. I remember it was a beautiful, bright sunny spring day, without a cloud in the sky.

My mother, brother, sister, and myself took his death very hard, but the grief we felt faded away as time moved on. Although the sadness has paled with time, there hasn't been a day since my father's death that I haven't thought about him. So, after ten years, when I saw the book *The Wild Blue* by Stephen E. Ambrose at a local store, I bought the book with the intention of reading it as a tribute to, and in memory of, my father.

The Wild Blue tells the story of the 15th Army Air Force in Italy during World War II, and in particular, details the service of Lieutenant George S. McGovern, a B-24 pilot who flew 35 missions against Nazi Germany during the years 1944 to 1945. He, later of course, became a Senator from South Dakota and the Democratic candidate for President of the United States in the 1972 election. McGovern was assigned to the 455th Bomb Group, 741st Squadron. I knew my father had been stationed in Italy around the same time and decided to research his unit and squadron. My mother provided his discharge papers which led me to the 456th Bomb Group Association where, with much help from its members, I was able to gather the information for this book.

I found the 456th Bomb Group Association web site on the Internet at the address http://www.456thbombgroup.org. The web site details the history of the group, plus contains many photographs from their base near Stornara and Cerignola, Italy. After reading practically every word on the web site and scanning all of the pictures, I was frustrated because I had not found any information about my father or the crew with which he flew.

As a last resort, I posted a message on the web site's guestbook asking for information about the crew of the *Boojum,* the name the crew had given to the B-24 bomber they flew. Coincidentally, another son of a former crew member, Michael J. Dancisak, also posted a message on the web site's guestbook at nearly the same time. A member of the 456th Bomb Group Association and a former bombardier in the 745th Squadron, Robert W. Reichard, responded to my post with an email message.

The email follows:

Subject: 456th!
From: Bob Reichard
To: Dave Abner

I just checked my 456th BG History Book and it says your Father and five others bailed out over Yugoslavia 3 April 1944 after their plane "The Texas Ranger" was hit by Flak on a mission to Budapest. I was in the 745th BS, but I didn't get there until Oct 1944. I'm sure that Fred Riley our Historian will contact you.

From a Farm in the rolling hills of Eastern Pennsylvania,

Bob Reichard

Mr. Reichard's email supplied the keys that opened the doors to the answers to all my questions. He had mentioned the 456th Bomb Group History Book whose title is actual*ly*:

456th Bomb Group
1943 – Steed's Flying Colts – 1945

I didn't even know there was a 456th Bomb Group History Book. I immediately sent Mr. Reichard an email thanking him and started searching the Internet for a bookstore that might have a copy of the history book. I found one copy in a used book store in Minneapolis, Minnesota and promptly placed an order for the book.

The following day, I had another email from Fred H. Riley, the 456th Bomb Group Historian, who provided a list of my father's crew members. One name on the list, Howard Hartman, listed as the co-pilot, had an existing street and email address.

Suddenly, as Sherlock Holmes might say, "The game was afoot."

I had many questions, such as:

Why was the crew flying in *The Texas Ranger* instead of the *Boojum*?

Why did only six men of the ten member crew bail out that day?

How did the rest of the crew make it back safely?

Did all members of the crew survive the war?

But now I had some leads to follow. The history book arrived and had an account of the mission. I sent Howard Hartman an email and he promptly responded. Mr. Hartman gladly told me the story of that April day in 1944, and put me in contact with Michael J. Dancisak, son of Technical Sergeant George L. Dancisak, the flight engineer, and with

Hans Halberstadt, son of 2nd Lieutenant Milton H. Halberstadt, the crew's navigator. Mr. Hartman also mentioned that he thought Edward L. DeMent, one of the crew's gunners, was still alive and living in Florida. I looked up Mr. DeMent's address on the Internet and sent him a letter of introduction, asking him for his story. Mr. DeMent wrote back and told me if I came to the 456th Bomb Group Association reunion that year in New Orleans, he would tell me his story.

I joined the 456th Bomb Group Association as an associate member and attended their reunion in May of 2003 in New Orleans. There, Howard Hartman, Edward DeMent, Michael Dancisak, and I spent several days and nights together. Edward DeMent gave me a copy of his book, *Sargent for You the War is Over*, which details the April 3rd mission and his experiences as a German prisoner of war.

The text of the book that follows is a compilation of all the facts and stories gathered over the better part of two years. I have to wholeheartedly thank Howard Hartman and Edward DeMent for supplying detailed eye witness accounts of their experiences on April 3, 1944 and their time spent in German prisoner of war camps. I must also give many thanks to Michael J. Dancisak, Ph.D, Tulane University for providing copies of photographs that his father George L. Dancisak took while serving in Italy during World War II. Most of the pictures in this book were supplied by Mr. Dancisak from his father's collection. I must also extend my heartfelt thanks to Hans Halberstadt who sent me copies of his father's, Milton H. Halberstadt's, navigator log book and several letters his father had received from other crewmen about his war experiences. And finally, I owe a debt of gratitude to Mr. Reichard, without whom this book would never have been started.

These five people made this book possible. As the lowly scribe, I have only put down on paper the stories and memories they freely shared with me. It is their story, and they are my heroes.

Author's note:

I have taken several liberties with the narrative in the book. First, all of the conversations attributed to the characters in the story are the invention of the author. My purpose was to make the text more enjoyable for the reader and to bring to life the members of the crew of the B-24H Heavy Bomber *Boojum*. The events in the book, however, did actually happen as described. Secondly, I have paraphrased in places, the words of Howard Hartman and Edward DeMent, the two surviving crew members, taken from the stories they provided me in their emails, letters, conversations, and from Mr. DeMent's book. I am sure they will forgive my acts of plagiarism, because this story is best told with the words of the men who were there.

David F. Abner
February 2004

This book is dedicated to the crew of the B-24H Heavy Bomber Boojum and their families.

"Monday morning, April 3, 1944 was like the past days, cloudy and overcast. We never dreamed that there was going to be a mission today."

Sgt. Edward L. DeMent

Top row left to right: Pilot Emil Laszewski, Co-Pilot Howard Hartman, Engineer George Dancisak, Navigator Milton Halberstadt, and Bombardier Edward Bonham.
Bottom row left to right: Tail Gunner Edward Thompson, Radio Operator Samuel Fischler, Nose Gunner Edward DeMent, Ball Turret Gunner Frederick Abner. Top Turret Gunner Reinaldo Garza.

Photograph provided by Howard Hartman

Chapter 1

Monday morning, April 3, 1944 was cloudy and overcast in the predawn light, just like the past several days. Nobody dreamed there would be a mission today. But the jeep stopped in front of their tent and the officer in charge of quarters, commonly known as the *CQ*, unceremoniously announced to the five sleeping men within that they were to fly again today. It was 4:30 am.

The five men stirred slowly from their cots and began to dress in their fatigues, without a single word being uttered. This was the fifth mission for these men in the past seven days. They all were tired and feeling the strain of so many combat missions in such a short time. No one had enjoyed a full night's sleep for the past week. And they couldn't help but notice the empty cot that sat in one corner of the tent.

In another part of the tent city that had been constructed in an olive grove, the four officers of the crew of aircraft tail number 42-52292 were also awakened in the same unceremonious way. They also dressed mostly in silence.

T/Sgt. George L. Dancisak with crew tents in background
Photograph provided by Michael J. Dancisak

The nine men, four officers and five enlisted men, all in their late teens or early twenties, made up the crew of a B-24H bomber which had affectionately been named *Boojum*. The name was the brainchild of the crew's navigator, 2nd Lt. Milton H. Halberstadt. Hal, as he was referred to by his fellow officers, had been an artist before the war in Cambridge, Massachusetts. He had suggested the name *Boojum* during the crew's stay in North Africa prior to their arrival in Italy. In the Lewis Carroll poem, *Hunting of the Snark*, *Boojum* was a mythical monster. Whoever looked upon the *Boojum* would *"softly and suddenly vanish away."* For a heavy bomber, vanquishing enemy fighters in this manner would certainly be advantageous.

The seemingly strange name was not lost on the six enlisted men of the crew who had looked up the word *Boojum* and found the word might also refer to a Chinese dragon. Soon a fierce looking Chinese dragon, snorting smoke and flame and the word *Boojum*, was painted on the right side of the aircraft's nose. No one seemed to mind the duality of meanings invoked by the aircraft's new name.

Boojum Nose Art, duplicated on a scarf
Photograph provided by Michael J. Dancisak

In this way, the plane now belonged to both the officers and non-commissioned officers of the crew. And the crew loved their *Boojum*. The crew had been assigned together at Mountain Home Field outside of Boise, Idaho on September 1, 1943, and had trained together there, and at Muroc Field, now Edwards Air Force Base, in California, 80 miles east of Los Angeles. The flight training lasted three months. On December 24, 1943 they had taken a train to San Francisco to pick up their brand new, shining B-24H Liberator at Hamilton Field. The crew had waited a long time for that to happen.

The B-24H was the state-of-the-art bomber being produced in late 1943. The bomber had a top speed of 300 miles per hour, could fly at an altitude of 30,000 feet, and had a range of 2,200 miles making it the fastest, highest flying, and longest range bomber produced in World War II up to that time.

There were ten crew positions; in addition to the pilot and co-pilot, the nose cabin held the bombardier and navigator positions, the flight deck behind the cockpit had positions for the radio operator and flight engineer, and there were four gun turrets. The turrets were located in the nose, tail, a top turret above the flight deck just behind the cockpit, and a bottom turret called the ball turret because it was shaped like a large Plexiglas ball. Additional gun placements were at the two waist windows cut in the fuselage halfway between the wings and the tail section. The waist guns were manned by the flight engineer and radio operator when under fighter attack. The navigator also had a Plexiglas observation dome located on top of the nose between the cockpit and the nose turret. The most innovative feature of the B-24 was its Davis wing, designed by David Davis at the Consolidated Aircraft Corporation in San Diego, which gave the aircraft incredible lift and payload capacity.

From San Francisco, they had flown the aircraft in hops across the country. First stopping in Palm Springs where a wealthy, local businessman invited the crew to play a round of golf on his private course. Next they flew to Midland, Texas where a sudden snow storm kept the plane grounded for three days, and then on to Kansas City for a few more days.

Other B-24 crews with their aircraft had also made it to Kansas City. All the crews and planes were members of the 456th Bomb Group (Heavy) under the command of Colonel Thomas W. Steed, from Etowah, Tennessee, a graduate of the U.S. Military Academy at West Point, class of 1928. Colonel Steed was a *soldier's soldier* and was highly respected by the men he commanded. He was a first class pilot and would end up being the lead pilot on over one third of all missions flown by the 456th Bomb Group during World War II.

The Bomb Group was made up of four squadrons, the 744th, 745th, 746th, and 747th and pilot 2nd Lieutenant Emil S. (Jeff) Laszewski's crew was assigned to the 745th Squadron. Laszewski was a tall and strongly built man from Depue, Illinois who had no trouble manhandling the control wheel of a B-24 Liberator.

The bomb group was part of the 15th Army Air Force. They were headed to the Mediterranean Theater of Operations (MTO) to form up at a base near Tunis in North

Africa. There they would wait for the advanced ground crews to finish constructing a runway in the newly liberated Foggia area of southern Italy. Once the runway was completed, the bomb group would fly into Italy to begin operations against the German war infrastructure.

As the officers sat around a table in the officer's mess, 2nd Lieutenant Milton H. Halberstadt turned to the co-pilot, 2nd Lt. Howard N. Hartman, and said,

"Howard, look over there. Isn't that the pilot of *The Texas Ranger*?"

Hartman, a tall, handsome, and well built young man from Shelby, Ohio stared across the dining room at the two men. He looked back at Halberstadt and replied,

"Yep, can't you tell? That guy always walks around wearing those pearl handled six-shooters, like he thinks he's in a western movie. And I believe that is his father with him in the cowboy hat. Remember, he came out to Muroc Field to visit once?"

Halberstadt grunted and said sarcastically,

"Right and this is supposed to be a classified deployment. I guess blood is thicker than security . . ."

From Kansas City the crew flew to Memphis, and then on to West Palm Beach, Florida. After a day resting and getting the plane refueled, they took off from West Palm Beach toward the island of Trinidad in the Caribbean.

After getting airborne, pilot 2nd Lieutenant Emil S. Laszewski, known as Jeff to the other officers of the crew, turned to Hartman and said,

"Howard, I can't get the engine cowl flaps to close."

The cowl flaps are doors cut into the bottom of each engine housing. The cowl flaps are opened when the plane's engines are idling on the ground to help cool the engines. Once airborne, the cowl flaps are closed.

Hartman reached down to his left and tried throwing the four engine cowl flap switches. Nothing happened.

"Jeff, it's no good. Maybe George can figure it out."

Laszewski keyed the intercom and called,

"Sergeant Dancisak, come up to the cockpit."

Technical Sergeant George Dancisak, the flight engineer from Whiting, Indiana, was short in stature but long on his understanding of the functioning of the aircraft. George had been trained on aircraft mechanics at the Ford Plant in Willow Run, Michigan and knew the workings of a B-24H inside and out. After being advised of the problem, he flipped the switches back and forth a few times with no effect.

"Sir, it is very unlikely that all four of these switches are malfunctioning. The problem has to be somewhere else. I think we ought to head back to the field."

Laszewski called the control tower and requested an emergency landing. However, he was told he couldn't land with a full load of fuel and would have to circle around out over the Atlantic Ocean until he burned off most of the aircraft fuel supply.

After George returned to his station amid ship, Staff Sergeant Frederick G. Abner, Jr., the ball turret gunner from Alexandria, Virginia, asked Dancisak about the problem. Abner had worked as an electrician's apprentice before the war, and was also trained as an aircraft mechanic at the Willow Run plant. During non-combat flights, he rode in the waist area of the bomber rather than in the cramped ball turret.

After hearing Dancisak's description of the problem, Abner said,

"Well, this is a brand new aircraft and so far we haven't had any problems. I guess its better we find out about the engine cowl flaps now instead of when we're overseas."

After Laszewski and Hartman made repeated tries of moving the engine cowls while flying the plane in circles, the cowl flaps finally closed.

The pilot and co-pilot did some quick calculations in the cockpit and decided they had just enough fuel to reach the field in Trinidad. The decision was made to try it and the plane was turned onto the correct heading.

Fred Abner turned to George Dancisak and said,

"George, you think we have enough fuel left to get to Trinidad."

Dancisak shrugged and said,

"Let's hope so, I don't think this crate will float very long."

Up in the cockpit, they were also concerned about the fuel as they dodged the ever-increasing thunderheads that built up quickly as the afternoon wore on across the wide expanse of the Caribbean. As the plane touched down on the runway in Trinidad, the number one engine began to sputter from lack of fuel. Hartman and Laszewski looked at each other and then broke out in smiles.

"Let's not tell the rest of the crew that we just landed on fumes." Laszewski quipped.

"I think they already know." Hartman replied.

The rest of the crew consisted of bombardier 2nd Lt. Edward C. Bonham from Eastern Pennsylvania, radio operator Sgt. Samuel Fischler from Brooklyn, New York, nose gunner Sgt. Edward L. DeMent from Chicago, top turret gunner S/Sgt. Reinaldo C. Garza from New Mexico, and tail turret gunner S/Sgt. Edward O. Thompson from Georgia. Halberstadt, Thompson, and Bonham were married. Bonham's wife had followed him from base to base while he was in training. He was handsome and she was very pretty and they made a fine couple, but now they would be separated by distance and war.

Fischler was a heavy set man who was loud and boisterous, some would say obnoxious, but he was a very funny guy who kept the crew loose with laughter.

DeMent was the youngest member of the crew. He had just graduated from high school and had joined up as soon as he had passed his eighteenth birthday.

Thompson was a tall, quiet country boy from the hills of Georgia. He spoke very infrequently, but had a quick wit and often surprised the crew with a biting one-liner.

From Trinidad, after the cowl flaps were adjusted, they flew to Belem and then to Natal, Brazil. Natal was the closest land point between South America and Africa. After a day's rest the crew flew the long hop across the southern Atlantic to Dakar, North Africa during the evening and night of January 18, 1944. This was the longest leg of the journey and severely tested 2nd Lt. Halberstadt's skill as a navigator. Hal took frequent sightings through the navigational port located on the top of the nose of the aircraft just in front of the cockpit. With a few minor course corrections Halberstadt successfully navigated the plane into the field at Dakar.

From Dakar, the crew flew on to Marrakech, Morocco and then Telerema, Algeria. Then it was off to Oudna, Tunisia, just outside of Tunis. There the crew waited several weeks while the ground crews, which had arrived earlier in the Foggia area of Italy by troop ship, completed the construction of a runway that would be wide enough and long enough to support the B-24 bomber. The ground crews had taken over a German fighter base located between Stornara and Cerignola which had been abandoned as the invading American and British army units advanced up the boot of Italy.

The rest of the B-24 bombers that made up the 456th Bomb Group assembled outside of Tunis as the work continued on the new airstrip in Italy. When the crew of the *Boojum* arrived at Oudna, there were already several other aircraft from the group on the ground. Bombers continued to straggle in over the next week. Some were delayed at various points with mechanical problems and others had started their trek across the ocean at later dates. By January 29, 1944, all aircraft had arrived with the exception of one. This was *The Texas Ranger*.

"Maybe the *great Texan* had to fly his father back to the ranch first," Halberstadt noted sarcastically.

Finally, on February 1, 1944, the runway was completed and the group took off from Tunisia for Italy where they landed and began preparing for combat operations. And now, the crew of the *Boojum* would begin the greatest adventure of their young lives.

The Texas Ranger managed to straggle into Italy several weeks later.

THE END OF THE RIDE . . . 456th ARRIVES IN ITALY.

Photograph from the 456th Bomb Group Newsletter, January 1944.

Chapter 2

Combat operations (missions) began on February 10, 1944 and continued through March and into April. The crew of the *Boojum* flew their first mission on February 17, 1944, group mission #2 to Grottoferrata, Italy, to bomb a German command post.

It was Ed DeMent's birthday. Ed had a passing thought that the flak that was exploding all around the aircraft looked like fireworks in celebration. Then a fighter made a pass firing its machine guns at the bomber. As DeMent returned fire, he couldn't help but wonder why this was happening. Why two men who had never met or exchanged an unkind word were trying to kill each other. Ed, as well as the rest of the crew, had just come face to face with the reality of war.

At first the missions were short ones to targets in Nazi held Italy. But as the crews gained experience and confidence, targets in Austria, Romania, Bulgaria, and Yugoslavia were also bombed by the 456th Bomb Group. During this time six aircraft and crews out of the original 64 were lost. A number of other crews had lost crewmen due to wounds from flak, enemy fighters, and frostbite. Sgt. Samuel Fischler had developed frostbite around the edges of his oxygen mask from standing at the open waist window while operating the waist machine gun. He would miss a number of missions while recovering.

These losses and injuries provided an opportunity for enlisted men, particularly gunners, to fly additional missions, almost whenever they wanted. There always seemed to be available gun positions due to attrition or sickness. This was partially due to the fact that crews lived in tents with little or no heat except what they could jury-rig themselves. And the Italian winter was cold and wet. Many missions had been scrubbed due to bad or deteriorating weather conditions.

Abner, DeMent, and Garza all flew as substitute gunners on extra missions. Garza was killed on March 19, 1944 during group mission #16 to Steyr, Austria while flying in a plane named *The Paper Doll*. Steyr was socked in with cloud cover so the secondary target at Klagenfurt, Austria was bombed.

Garza had been manning the top turret when a rocket from a German fighter hit the plane, and the plane exploded in mid-air. He was not flying with his normal crew because there were shortages of personnel, so the gunners were temporarily spread out to help cover the shortages. (And that is why there was an empty cot in the enlisted men's tent on the morning of April 3, 1944).

Sgt. Edward DeMent was also flying in another aircraft as the nose gunner that day and watched helplessly as the plane that Garza was in went down. He had not been able to see whether anyone had bailed out of *The Paper Doll*. Then suddenly, DeMent was knocked unconscious when a flak fragment penetrated the nose turret. He was revived before the plane returned to base and suffered shrapnel cuts over his right eye and forehead for which he received the first of his three Purple Heart's.

Several days later, DeMent asked Jeff Laszewski if he could man the top turret which had been Garza's position. He felt it was less exposed to flak then the nose turret. Laszewski gave DeMent the okay knowing that they would be getting a substitute gunner to replace Garza on subsequent missions who could man the nose turret. But in reality, there were no safe positions on a B-24 over enemy territory.

DeMent had 24 missions to his credit. He had flown on every mission possible in an effort to finish his tour so he could get back to the States in time to take his high school sweetheart to the prom. Fred Abner had flown 17 missions by April 3rd, many of them as a substitute ball turret gunner. His motivation was to escape the boredom of camp life and to get the required missions behind him.

Although Abner had not been credited with shooting down an enemy fighter, he had shot at several. On one mission, the bomb bay doors somehow became detached from a B-24 flying above and in front of his plane. As the doors fell, they aligned end-to-end, and to Fred they appeared to be the wings of a German fighter. He immediately fired a burst of rounds from his ball turret machine guns blasting the bomb bay doors out of the sky, to the unbridled amusement of his crewmates. Thus, S/Sgt. Frederick G. Abner, Jr. was the only man in the 456th Bomb Group ever credited with a confirmed kill on a pair of bomb bay doors.

The crew of the *Boojum* had only flown nine missions together. The officers, flight engineer, and radio operator were restricted from flying extra missions, unless ordered to, because they would not be replaceable for months if lost. So their missions were necessarily tied to their assigned aircraft.

On the morning of April 3, 1944, as the crewmen stumbled around in the predawn darkness of their tents getting dressed and wondering whether there would, or would not be a mission today, Colonel Steed and the rest of the operations staff and planners were preparing to fly the third mission in a row over Yugoslavia to another Balkan capital.

When the crewmen finished getting dressed, they gathered outside their tents and waited for an uncovered, drab green army truck to come by and pick them up. Each man climbed up on the rear bumper and swing themselves into the back of the truck over the tail gate, and sat on one of the benches that ran along each side. When the benches were full, crewmen sat on the floor. The trucks stopped at the chow hall tents where a breakfast of powdered milk, powdered eggs, potatoes, white bread toast, and industrial strength coffee was served. A permanent chow hall was under construction at the time and would not be ready for several months.

Queuing up at the Chow Hall Tent
Photograph provided by Michael J. Dancisak

New Chow Hall under Construction
Photograph provided by Michael J. Dancisak

Following the hastily eaten breakfast, briefings were held for the various crew components at the 456th Bomb Group Headquarters building and surrounding tents. The airstrip was laid out south to north and the Group Headquarters area was in the Southwest corner of the airstrip. The pilot and co-pilot would attend the main briefing which was always an anxious time, waiting for the briefing officer to uncover the map of southern Europe which would show the path that today's bombing mission would take over enemy territory. There were no missions that were *milk runs*. But missions to Austria, especially to targets near Vienna, were the most feared because of the heavy concentration of flak guns and enemy fighters.

When the map was unveiled, it revealed a red line pointing across the coast of Yugoslavia toward the Hungarian capital of Budapest. The target was the main railroad marshalling yards on the outskirts of the city.

Hartman turned to Laszewski and whispered,

"Jeff, this is the third day in a row we're flying the same route."

Laszewski nodded and replied,

"Yeah, the Krauts will eventually get wise to us if we keep flying there."

The rest of the briefing was taken up with the particulars of the flight pattern, weather conditions, and expected opposition from fighters and flak over the target area. When the meeting broke up, Colonel Steed, who would be flying the lead plane today, walked over to Hartman and Laszewski and said,

"Lieutenant Laszewski, can I see you for a moment?" Jeff Laszewski had recently been promoted from 2nd to 1st Lieutenant.

Laszewski and Steed moved to the side, away from the line of men exiting the briefing room. Hartman said,

"Jeff, I'll wait for you outside," then turned and walked away.

Colonel Steed waited until most of the men had left the room and then turned to Laszewski.

"Jeff, I have a favor to ask of you. You know the crew that flies *The Texas Ranger*?"

Laszewski knew alright,

"You mean the crew that was a month late arriving here and has never made it over the target yet in nine tries? Yeah, I know them."

Colonel Steed smiled and continued,

"Well, they claim the plane is unfit to fly in combat and each time they have aborted a mission it was because of a mechanical difficulty. The ground crew swears there is nothing wrong with the plane. I want you to take it up today so we can prove that the plane is okay and the crew is not."

Laszewski considered for and moment and said,

"Colonel, I have the good crew and the best aircraft in the squadron. They go hand in hand. If we have to fly a different plane, it could affect our performance. The men won't be happy with the change and it could affect their morale."

Steed put his hand on Laszewski's shoulder,

"Jeff, I promise, just this once, fly another aircraft and you can have your old plane back for the duration after the mission."

Laszewski turned and looked directly at Colonel Steed. There was no point in continuing the discussion.

"Yes sir."

Steed slapped Laszewski on the back and replied,

"Thanks Jeff, see you after the mission." Then Colonel Steed remembered something else. "Oh, and one more thing, your men will find some extra boxes loaded on the plane near the waist windows. The boxes are full of aluminum tinsel like the kind you hang on Christmas trees."

Laszewski gave Steed a quizzical look. Colonel Steed smiled and continued,

"Jeff, the tinsel has been used by the 8th Army Air Force in England to jam enemy radar during the bomb runs over Germany. They swear it throws off the aim of the flak guns. Since you are flying the deputy lead plane of box three today, which puts you near the middle of the formation, I thought I'd let you try it out. Just have your radio operator and flight engineer throw handfuls out of the waist windows during the bomb run."

"Okay", answered Laszewski, "We can use all the help fooling those AA batteries we can get. I'll inform the crew."

"Good luck Jeff," Colonel Steed said to end the conversation.

Laszewski smiled and gave the thumbs up signal, then turned and walked out of the Headquarters building where Hartman was waiting. When he told Howard of the change in aircraft, the co-pilot was visibly upset.

"Jeff, you know how much the crew loves their *Boojum*. They aren't going to take this well. Hell, I 'm not going to take this well!"

It was now 6:30 am.

The rest of the crew was involved in their own briefings. Navigators, bombardiers, and gunners all had their separate meetings to discuss various aspects of the mission. Navigators were briefed on the route into and out of the target, locations of known flak gun concentrations which were to be flown around, and possible emergency landing sites. Bombardiers were briefed on the tonnage and the numbers of bombs loaded in the bomb bay, and were shown aerial photos from recon flights of the target area to help them identify the targets. The other six members of the crew manned guns when in combat and were briefed on the numbers and types of enemy aircraft expected to be encountered. In addition, the radio operator was given the frequencies and radio protocol for the day, and the flight engineer was advised of the amount of fuel loaded in the wing tanks.

After the briefing, the crewmen went to the supply tent to receive their heated flight suits, headsets, and parachutes. The B-24 Liberator was not heated and temperatures at 25,000 feet often reached 40 or more degrees below zero. The flight suits could be plugged into AC outlets throughout the aircraft that heated the suits. Rheostats at the outlets provided a means of controlling the temperature. But no amount of heating could make those temperatures comfortable.

Once the crews received their equipment, they gathered together and waited for the trucks to transport them to the airplane. Laszewski broke the news of the aircraft change to the rest of the crew and discussed the use of the tinsel. No one was happy about the change, but the enlisted men were quiet, in deference to the officers.

Navigator 2nd Lt. Hal Halberstadt was the only one to voice his opinion. As the four officers stood together he muttered.

"Jeff, it's bad enough that I am married to a Hungarian and we are going to bomb Budapest, but now we have to fly in an unfamiliar plane!"

2nd Lt. Edward Bonham, the bombardier, replied,

"Hal, it'll be okay, just get me close enough to unload those babies from the bomb bay!"

To that Halberstadt replied,

"Don't worry Ed. I'll get us there and back. You just make sure you don't hit the wrong target. I still have relatives and in-laws in Budapest."

Chapter 3

Once the crew was dropped off at the cul-de-sac like pad where *The Texas Ranger* was parked, George Dancisak and Fred Abner walked around the plane doing a pre-flight inspection and then followed the rest of the crew, who had already climbed into the plane through the bomb bay doors and went to their stations. S/Sgt. Edward Thompson had to crawl from the bomb bay catwalk through the narrow tunnel of the rear fuselage to get to his position in the tail turret. Likewise, Bonham and Halberstadt had to crawl under the flight deck and cockpit to reach their cramped positions in the nose. Sgt. Edward DeMent climbed up to the top turret where he stood inside the glass dome on a platform just behind the pilot and co-pilot seats. Sgt. Samuel Fischler sat down at the radio operator's position next to T/Sgt. George Dancisak who, as the flight engineer, also had a seat.

Pre-flight inspection at Stornara Field, Italy 1944
Photograph provided by Michael J. Dancisak

During aerial combat, Dancisak and Fischler would man the guns protruding from the waist windows, one on either side of the aircraft. S/Sgt. Fred Abner could not yet squeeze into the tight quarters of the ball turret until the plane was in the air and the turret could be lowered. The ball turret was so small the gunner could not wear his parachute when inside. In addition, the ball turret gunner had to rely on a crewman to retract the turret in times of crisis. Those limitations made the ball turret the most vulnerable position on the aircraft.

Abner and Dancisak were both trained as aircraft mechanics, with George being the flight engineer and Abner acting as the backup. Having two members of the crew trained in aircraft mechanics was a bonus and had proved invaluable during a mission on March 22, 1944 over Verona, Italy. The target had been obscured by clouds, so a secondary target, the railroad marshalling yards at Bologna and Rimini, was bombed instead. Just after the bombs were away, a flak shell burst beneath the still opened bomb bay doors, blowing the doors away and rupturing two fuel lines. The lines ran along the side of the fuselage through valves that allowed the flight engineer to control the fuel supply to each engine. Dancisak had immediately jumped over to the worst fuel leak. He yelled to Fischler,

"Sam, pull the ball turret up and get Abner out, I need some help here."

As Fischler reached for the levered mechanism that would bring the ball turret back into the belly of the plane, Dancisak tried to plug the first leak. The fuel pipe was spraying gasoline all over his flight suit. George felt super cold fuel burning his chest, but he knew he couldn't stop working until the leak was plugged.

Fred Abner climbed out of the turret, took in the scene, and grabbed a nearby rag that was lying at the base of one of the waist guns. He slowly moved out onto the damaged catwalk that ran across the bomb bay area. The bomb bay doors were gone and below the catwalk nothing was left. Air rushed in and violently whipped around the damaged fuselage. Abner grabbed the vertical beam that supported the catwalk and reached out over the now open space, where he could see the ground rushing by below, and pushed the rag into the hole in the second leaking fuel line. Cold gasoline ran down his left arm, burning his arm and left side of his torso.

Laszewski sent Hartman back to access the situation. When Howard returned he reported,

"The bomb bay is gone. George is working on one leak without a shirt on and he is soaked in gasoline. Abner is hanging halfway out of the ship holding a rag in another line. We better drop to a lower altitude before they both pass out from lack of oxygen."

The plane had already lost altitude due to the lack of fuel to two of the engines which were running erratically. Laszewski continued to descend to 10,000 feet so the crew could go off of oxygen.

Abner and Dancisak finally got both leaks under control. The two fuel starved engines began to run normally again. Both men suffered from frostbite caused by the cold fuel.

George Dancisak was by far the worst off and would carry scars on his chest for the rest of his life. Neither man missed any missions, but instead toughed it out even though they were in pain from their burns.

That had been a rough mission, the worst so far.

Today, as the crew was going through their pre-flight checks, a replacement gunner arrived. Because S/Sgt. Reinaldo C. Garza had been killed on an earlier mission, he was being replaced on each new mission by a substitute gunner. The new arrival announced himself as S/Sgt. Howard Kiefer. He was told to man the nose turret.

Fischler conducted a radio check and then a check of the aircraft's intercom to make sure all crew members could hear and be heard. During the flight, a check of the crew via the intercom would be necessary every 10 minutes. At the altitude the plane flew, temperatures ranged between minus 40 and minus 50 degrees. A man could pass out and suffocate if the moisture from his breath caused his oxygen supply tube to freeze shut. So the intercom checks were a necessary survival routine.

A red flare shot from the control tower alerted the crews to begin the mission. As the plane started to taxi into the lineup of B-24s heading for the main runway, George asked,

"Fred, how many missions does this make for you?"

"This is my eighteenth," Abner answered'

"That must make you the man with the most missions," George said.

"Nope, I think Ed DeMent has me beat. Hey Ed, how many missions you got now?" Abner yelled up to the top turret.

DeMent dropped down out of the turret and joined George, Fred, and Sam in the cramped waist area.

"This is my twenty-fifth and I am out of here after this one, R&R on the Island of Capri, and I can't wait!"

The men of the 15th Army Air Force were required to fly 50 missions. Missions above a certain longitudinal parallel were counted as two missions. After five missions, you were rewarded with the Air Medal. After 15 you received an Oak Leaf Cluster for your Air Medal, and another Oak Leaf Cluster for each additional ten missions. After 25 missions, you were given leave for two weeks on the Isle of Capri where the Army had procured local hotel rooms for the purpose of entertaining the troops. Getting to Capri was an intermediate goal of all crewmen, with the main goal of completing the 50 missions necessary to qualify for a stateside assignment.

"Yeah, you're the luckiest guy I know, flying all those extra missions," Samuel Fischler said. "But don't you think you are tempting fate a bit too much?"

"I got to get back to my girl." DeMent replied.

Just then Laszewski's voice boomed over the intercom,

"Get in position for take off."

The plane made its last turn and started lumbering down the runway. To Howard Hartman in the co-pilot's seat, it always seemed like the plane would never get up enough ground speed to lift off. With a full load of fuel and 500 or 1,000 pound bombs onboard, the B-24H would barely attain enough ground speed to get up in the air by the end of the runway. But somehow they always made it. And today was no exception. The plane gradually, but grudgingly, gained altitude and soon was circling the landing strip waiting for the other planes in their group to form up.

The formation of bombers was made up of boxes of seven planes each that flew in a close formation. This provided the most protection from enemy fighters. The lead plane was followed by a plane slightly behind and below each wing forming a V, followed by a second three plane V formation. The seventh plane in the box would be behind the other six planes lined up with the lead plane. The lead plane of the group was designated as position *Able 1*, the plane to the right *Able 2*, to the left *Able 3*, and so on to the last plane *Able 7*. The second box, to the right of the lead box and slightly behind, was designated *Baker 1-7*. And the other boxes in the formation were designated *Charlie1-7*, *Dog 1-7*, *Fox 1-7*, etc. Most formations were divided into two units of two or three boxes each. The second unit of the formation flew one or two thousand feet below the first unit to minimize prop wash effects.

An enemy fighter would face the maximum number of guns if attacking a close formation. Most times, fighters kept their distance from a well formed formation and went after stragglers. The lead plane and the last plane of a group, dubbed "tail end Charlie", were the most vulnerable to fighter attack. If a plane dropped out of formation and fell behind over enemy territory, the fighters descended on the crippled aircraft to finish it off.

The lineup of B-24 Liberators continued to take off while those already airborne circled the field waiting for all planes to get to their assigned position in the formation. By 9:00 a.m. the group formation was together. Laszewski's plane was deputy lead of box three or flying in the *Charlie 2* position today. When the formation was formed up properly, the lead navigator gave the lead pilot, Colonel Steed, the compass heading and the bomber group turned toward the Italian coast, the Adriatic Sea, and on toward Yugoslavia.

Flying in loose Formation over the Adriatic Sea
Photograph provided by Michael J. Dancisak

Chapter 4

Milton Halberstadt and Edward Bonham always felt the most vulnerable during takeoffs and landings. The nose of the aircraft consisted mainly of clear Plexiglas. Most times, the navigator and bombardier would move out of the nose cabin during takeoffs and landings and sit in the waist area. The two men moved back to their positions in the nose as soon as the plane was safely airborne.

In front and above the nose cabin was the nose turret, now occupied by Howard Kiefer. Behind and above were the pilot and co-pilots positions in the cockpit, whose legs and feet, as they moved the rudder pedals, could be seen from the navigator/bombardier position in the nose. The Norden bombsight took up most of the room behind the glass dome and the two men found it hard to move in the cramped area. Halberstadt had a small shelf protruding from the fuselage for his maps and navigation charts. He was furiously working with a pencil, protractor, and ruler.

"Hal, what are you doing, we already have the coordinates for the flight to the target?" Bonham asked.

Hal looked up from his work and said,

"Ed, this is the first mission that we haven't flown in *Boojum*. That plane never failed us. For the first time in ten missions, I am plotting our return trip in advance. Call me superstitious, but I got a bad feeling about this one!"

"Hal, you have a bad feeling about all of them!" Bonham smiled and replied.

Halberstadt went back to work on his return flight path and muttered under his breath,

"Yeah, but this one doesn't feel right."

The crew had been together for seven months, and by now were a tight combat unit; each man proficient at his job and each man had complete confidence in the others. Some true friendships had formed. The crew began to bond back in Idaho when they had rented bicycles in Boise. The crew spent the day riding around the town, shopping, eating at the local soda fountain, and finally meeting in the town park. A local reporter, driving by in his car, saw them riding around together as a crew and thought it would make a good story. He interviewed the crew and the story was published the next day in the Boise newspaper.

Two Noses Geo & Abner

George Dancisak and Fred Abner in Boise, 1943
Photograph provided by Michael J. Dancisak

Later, at Muroc Field in the Mojave Desert, the crew flew almost everyday, practicing formation flying, navigation, bomb runs, and gunnery. It was hot and dry, the barracks were spartan and dust and snakes were everywhere.

Muroc Field, now Edwards Air Force Base, California
Photograph provided by the 456th Bomb Group Association

The crew got passes whenever they could to escape the hell hole of Muroc, and took the bus to Los Angeles some 80 miles west. The men would split up and go their separate ways, but one night the enlisted men agreed to meet at the world famous watering hole, the *Hollywood Canteen*.

Samuel Fischler, George Dancisak, and Fred Abner found themselves in a mock jail in Long Beach.

Fischler, Dancisak, and Abner
Photograph provided by Michael J. Dancisak

They all finally made it to the *Hollywood Canteen* where they had a light dinner, drinks, traded stories, and collected autographs from movie stars until the canteen closed. George Dancisak took a pen and wrote the date, October 15, 1943 on a napkin and pocketed it for a keepsake.

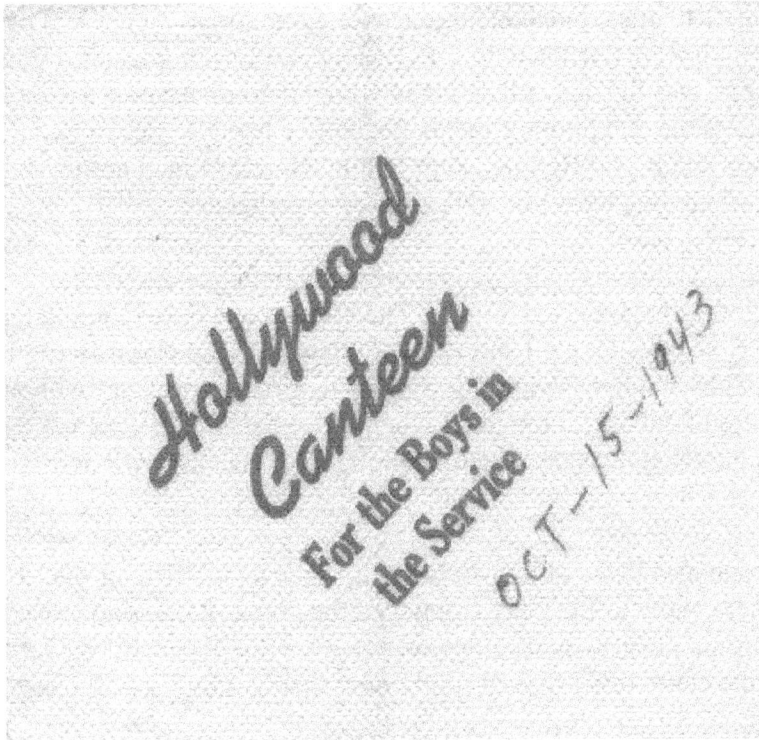

Photograph provided by Michael J. Dancisak

Howard Hartman and Jeff Laszewski would sometimes go to the theater in Los Angeles and one night went with Milton Halberstadt to *Errol Carrol's Night Club* which was another famous watering hole featuring lots of beautiful show girls.

It was another two and a half months before the crew traveled by train to pick up their brand new B-24H Liberator at Hamilton Field, outside of San Francisco. They arrived Christmas Day and were taken by jeep out across the tarmac to the plane. Everyone in the crew was thrilled and excited. They walked all around the plane looking it over and then each crewman climbed up through the bomb bay and went to his position. In a way, they were like children on Christmas morning.

"This is the biggest Christmas present I ever got!" Ed DeMent exclaimed.

Once in Italy, the officers lived together in one tent in the officer's area and the enlisted men lived in their tent in the enlisted man's area. Fraternization between officers and enlisted men was discouraged on the ground, but when together as a crew, military courtesy was relaxed. The only real distinction of rank on the aircraft was that the pilot was the captain of the ship.

The crew had gone together once to the little town of Cerignola just after they arrived in Italy. They found a confectionary shop downtown and purchased all the chocolate in the shop. The shop owner was so happy after such a large purchase that he actually cried.

Among the officers, Jeff Laszewski and Howard Hartman had become great friends. Likewise, among the enlisted men George Dancisak and Fred Abner had developed a true friendship, and both were friends with Ed DeMent and Ed Thompson. Dancisak, being the flight engineer, was the one enlisted man who had to interface with the officers regularly to discuss the condition of the plane, and he had also developed a friendship with Milton Halberstadt. Ed Bonham kept to himself and tended not to socialize with the other crewmen when they went out and caroused together.

Samuel Fischler had some basic hygiene issues. He didn't bathe regularly and often didn't change clothes for weeks at a time. The crew at one time took matters into their own hands and gave Fischler a GI shower, complete with industrial strength soap and scrub brushes. This changed his attitude and his hygiene improved. Although Fischler was not often sought out as a companion when the enlisted men were off duty, when he did accompany the others, he kept them laughing with his quick wit and sarcastic sense of humor.

Edward Thompson also had a quick wit but was the least likely to speak. He exuded the "tall cowboy" aura and was the Gary Cooper of the crew. Reinaldo Garza, being from a Hispanic background, generally went his own way. Still, his death on March 19th was a shock and was the cause of a sense of foreboding that had followed the crew on each mission since.

The plane was now flying over the Adriatic Sea on a course for the southern part of Yugoslavia. This was a familiar route since the mission of March 30th to Sofia, Bulgaria had brought them on the same heading and the mission of April 2nd (yesterday's mission) to Steyr, Austria had also started out over the Adriatic and Yugoslavia.

Because *The Texas Ranger* and Laszewski's crew were in the middle of the formation, only Edward Thompson in the tail gun position had a good view of the rest of the group. Today there were twenty nine planes that made the mission. Laszewski called Thompson over the intercom,

"Tail gunner, how is the group keeping up behind us?"

After a pause, Thompson came back with his usual witty response,

"Just like a gaggle of geese sir."

"Thompson, I am going to gaggle your goose if you don't give me a straight answer!" Laszewski ordered in a mock tone.

"Yes sir, there is a gaggle of bombers formed up nicely behind us, sir."

Laszewski and Hartman smiled at each other and Hartman quipped,

"What a country boy."

"Yeah from now on I think I'll call him *Jethro*."

The coast of Yugoslavia was now coming into view. The sky which had dawned gray and overcast was now deep blue, and the sun was shining brightly making the bombers clearly visible to anyone on the ground that might be looking skyward. From their current altitude of approximately 9000 feet, the waves breaking on the shoreline ahead were clearly visible. It had turned into a really nice day, so far . . .

Boojum, flying in formation over the Adriatic
Photograph provide by Michael J. Dancisak

Chapter 5

The formation was just passing through the 10,000 feet altitude level. Pilot Jeff Laszewski called over the intercom for the crew to go on oxygen. Each crew member was now in his combat position and slid the oxygen mask over his face. The masks included a microphone and each man also wore a headset for the intercom. Any conversation could now be heard by the whole crew. But there would not be much of that. It was time to get serious. They had crossed over into enemy territory.

The same actions were taking place in the twenty eight other aircraft. The nose, top, ball, and tail gunners were in their turrets scanning the sky for any sign of enemy fighters. The pilot and co-pilot also became more attentive to the sky around them. The flight engineer and radio operator were at their stations, but were ready to man the waist guns at the first sighting of an enemy fighter.

The lead navigator had given the lead pilot the compass heading for the initial point. The initial point was the point at which the pilot of the lead ship would turn the aircraft off the present course and onto the course directly toward the target. The lead navigator would advise the lead pilot as the group formation neared the initial point and tell the lead pilot when to turn the formation and what the new heading should be.

The bombardier was the only member of the Laszewski crew that was not busy at this time. Edward Bonham was enjoying the view out the nose of the plane. Hal Halberstadt was just writing in his log,

"10:05 Mostar, 10,000 feet, climbing . . ."

Bonham noticed some puffs of black smoke just ahead, and said without thinking,

"Hey, is it some kind of holiday down there, someone on the ground is shooting off fireworks."

"Lieutenant, that's not fireworks, that's flak!" Ed DeMent in the top turret said incredulously.

Halberstadt looked up from his log book. Suddenly a flak shell exploded just in front of the aircraft's nose. A hole opened up in the fuselage above Bonham and to the right of Kiefer in the nose turret. Halberstadt was knocked backward by a mighty blow to his chest.

Then all hell broke loose. The plane bucked upward and then started falling.

Laszewski and Hartman watched in disbelief as every gauge on their instrument panel dropped to zero. The number two engine was streaming smoke and sputtering erratically.

The plane dropped out of formation. Somehow, the other planes in the group managed to avoid *The Texas Ranger* as it dropped further below and behind.

Laszewski ripped off his oxygen mask and reached for the switch to feather the number two engine. Dancisak jumped up to the cockpit and reported,

"We've just lost all electrical power."

Hartman reached up and set the compass around 180 degrees to approximate their return heading. He turned in his seat and said,

"George, we had to feather number two."

Laszewski put the aircraft into a gentle turn and added,

"I am turning back toward home. The controls are really sluggish. This thing is flying like a pig."

Just then Bonham yelled,

"Hal's been hit, he's hurt bad. He's bleeding everywhere! I don't know what to do."

The fuse of the 88 mm flak shell had hit Halberstadt's flak jacket, careened off at a right angle, and lodged in the oil line of engine number two. Along the way, the fuse had also ripped opened Halberstadt's right hand. Halberstadt felt like he had been hit by a truck. He couldn't speak, could barely breathe, was barely conscious, and was doubled up in pain on the floor of the nose cabin.

The plane crossed back over the Adriatic. Laszewski was trying to level the plane but was losing the battle. He turned to Hartman,

"We can't make it back. We're losing altitude too fast."

"Let's salvo the bombs and see if that helps," Hartman suggested.

Dropping the twelve 500 pound bombs would surely lighten the load and perhaps give the aircraft enough lift to return to level flight. George Dancisak, who was still on the flight deck said,

"Without power, we can't open the bomb bay doors."

"George, can we drop the bombs through the doors?" Laszewski asked.

Dancisak paused a moment and replied,

"I don't see why not. The bombs aren't armed yet and they weigh enough to smash those doors wide open. Go for it skipper."

The plane was falling rapidly, a decision had to be made fast. Laszewski turned and yelled back to Fischler at his radio position,

"Fischler, get Abner out of the ball turret and both of you stand clear of the bomb bay. Let me know when you're done."

Fischler raised the ball turret manually and opened the hatch, tapped Fred on the shoulder, and helped him pull himself out through the opening. Fischler motioned Abner away from the bomb bay. He looked at Fischler and asked,

"Thanks Sam, we're hit bad aren't we?" Fischler nodded and yelled to let Laszewski know they were clear.

"The Germans must have moved some AA guns up on railroad cars. I guess we have flown one too many missions over Yugoslavia." Fischler added.

"Bonham, salvo all the bombs, now!" Laszewski ordered.

Bonham moved away from Halberstadt and reached for the lever beside the bombsite that would salvo the bombs. The bombs dropped, and with the wrenching sound of metal against metal tore open the bomb bay doors. Bent and dangling, flapping in the slipstream, the doors seemed to be hanging onto the fuselage by a thread.

In the cockpit, Laszewski and Hartman felt the plane rise up as the bombs fell away. This was a natural occurrence when so much weight left the plane at once, and happened on each bomb run when the bombs were released.

After a minute or so, Hartman asked,

"Jeff, we are flying better, aren't we?"

Laszewski waited several moments before he replied,

"Better, but we are still dropping. I don't think we can make it back. We didn't have enough altitude to start with."

"Yeah, I see we are not losing altitude as fast now, but we're still sinking," Hartman concurred.

Laszewski considered the situation and decided,

"Howard, I have to turn back over land again. If we have to bail the crew they won't survive in the water. Hell, I don't even know if any of them can swim!"

Again, Laszewski put the plane into a gentle turn back toward the coast.

Bonham called up to the flight deck,

"I really need some help down here with Hal."

George Dancisak was still on the flight deck watching the activity in the cockpit. The only instrument that was working was the magnetic compass which didn't depend on an electrical supply.

"We can throw out everything that's not nailed down including the waist guns. I am going down to check on Hal," He said. And with that he dropped down from the flight deck and crawled into the nose.

There wasn't enough room for three men in the nose section so Bonham let Dancisak push by him and then crawled out to the waist area and joined Fischler and Abner.

"Sir, how is Lieutenant Halberstadt?" Abner asked.

"Not good, he took some flak in the gut and his hand is bleeding everywhere. George is looking after him. I heard George say that we lost number two engine and all electrical power."

"Damn the luck. We should never have been in this airplane." Fischler cursed.

Hartman walked down from the cockpit to the waist.

"Guys, we have to throw everything we can out of the plane, we are still losing altitude," he said.

With that, Bonham, Abner, and Fischler started grabbing whatever was lying loose and tossing it down the opened bomb bay. Edward Thompson had remained at his post in the tail turret until this point and now he crawled out of his position dragging two ammo boxes filled with 50 caliber machine gun cartridge belts. He pushed them over the edge of the catwalk out of the bomb bay.

"We just turned back toward the Yugoslav coast," Thompson announced.

Fred Abner looked up from an ammo box he was dragging to the bomb bay and said,

"We are still airworthy. We should be heading back to Italy."

"I guess Lieutenant Laszewski doesn't think we'll make it," Thompson replied.

Bonham and Fischler were manhandling one of the waist guns toward the bomb bay, a cartridge belt still attached and dragging behind. The cartridge belt snagged a parachute strap and as the gun went out the bomb bay, the parachute fell through with it.

"Whoops, whose chute was that?" asked Abner.

"Must be George's, we all have ours on," Fischler said.

Fred Abner grabbed one of the boxes of aluminum tinsel and carried it over to the bomb bay.

"Guess we should have used this stuff sooner. It's not much good now," Abner said as he tossed the box out of the bomb bay.

Thompson grabbed the other box and heaved it out,

"Maybe some of the Slovaks can use this next Christmas."

In the cockpit, Laszewski and Hartman were watching the horizon. The plane was over the coast again, still loosing altitude, albeit at a much slower rate. George Dancisak climbed back up to the flight deck.

"Halberstadt is conscious, but he will never be able to jump." He reported. "I gave him some morphine to ease the pain and stopped as much of the bleeding as I could."

Just then, Abner came up behind Dancisak.

"George, your parachute slipped through the bomb bay when we were throwing out the guns." George shrugged. "I guess we better get this ship home then."

"Abner, have we thrown out everything we can dump," Hartman asked.

"Yes sir, unless we start dismantling the fuselage."

Dancisak and Abner moved off the flight deck. DeMent was still in the top turret scanning the sky for enemy fighters. A wounded plane was a sitting duck.

Dancisak looked at Abner and said,

"Fred, I have to get back and look after Hal." Motioning with his head toward the cockpit he continued, "Let's hope they can right this bird."

Abner nodded and replied,

"Yeah George, there isn't much else we can do that we haven't done already."

Dancisak crawled back to the nose and Abner moved to the waist area where Thompson, Bonham, and Fischler were standing.

The plane was now only several thousand feet above the deck. Laszewski looked at Hartman and said,

"Howard, it's hopeless, I can't gain any altitude. You better start jumping the crew."

Hartman nodded, unbuckled his seat belt, and headed toward the rear of the plane.

"Listen up!" He ordered, "We aren't going to make it fellows. We have to jump. Abner you go first."

Abner gave Hartman a questioning look for a moment, then moved over to the bomb bay, reached up and tightened the straps on his parachute, put his hand around the ripcord, squatted down and rolled forward as he had been taught out of the bomb bay.

S/Sgt. Frederick G. Abner, Jr., wearing a parachute
Photograph provided by David F. Abner

Hartman then told Thompson to go, followed by Fischler. Bonham then followed Fischler out the bomb bay. Hartman then walked back and reached up and grabbed DeMent's leg above him in the top turret.

"Ed, it's time to go."

DeMent dropped down from the turret, strapped on his parachute, and went to the bomb bay and squatted down. The wind was whipping past his face and the bomb bay doors where flapping back and forth in the wind. He hesitated for a moment. Hartman gave him a gentle nudge and out he went.

The plane was now only about one thousand feet above the green, hilly and rocky Yugoslavian farmland below. Hartman went back to the cockpit. Laszewski looked up at him as he came into the cabin and said,

"Howard, you better get out before it's too late. I can't jump with a wounded man aboard. I'll have to try to set it down somewhere."

"I'll stay and give you a hand at the controls," Hartman volunteered.

"George doesn't have a chute and he can give me a hand if I need it. Howard, get the hell out now, and that's an order," Laszewski said.

"Yes sir." Hartman paused, looked at his pilot, and said, "Good luck Jeff."

Howard Hartman pulled on his parachute, walked back to the bomb bay and jumped out.

Chapter 6

Howard Hartman had been trained to count ten seconds before pulling the ripcord to release the parachute. But with the plane so low, he counted off the ten seconds in less then three. The parachute started to deploy. He noticed the ground was coming up fast. The chute had barely opened and filled with air when he hit the ground. He pulled off the parachute pack and started collapsing the canopy. He looked up. *The Texas Ranger* was no longer losing altitude and in fact was starting to climb. The plane made a gentle turn and flew back toward him. Laszewski waggled the wings as it flew overhead and back toward the Adriatic and home.

Hartman was a big man at six foot three inches tall, and with his flight suit and parachute on weighed about 220 pounds. The combined weight of the five crewmen who jumped before him had not been enough to right the airplane. But once his big frame was out of the plane, that had done the trick. Now his thoughts were a jumbled mess.

He was happy the plane and Jeff would have a chance to make it back. He was happy he was alive after the jump. But he was not too happy about the group of partisans that had just pulled up in a truck on the nearby dirt road and stopped fifty yards in front of him. Four of them were coming across the field with their rifles raised.

Fred Abner felt the cold air rushing by, pulled the rip cord and was surprised at the violent jolt he felt when the parachute opened. He looked up and around and saw other parachutes opening some distance away. Abner could not believe this was happening. He was sure the plane could have made it back without the men having to bail out. Being the first to jump, he had no idea that it wasn't until Hartman jumped that the plane had straightened out. All he knew was that the plane was heading back to Italy without him.

He looked down and saw that he was headed for a field that was divided up into small fenced-in areas for livestock. The fences were constructed of stone. He was having trouble controlling the parachute in the cross wind. He landed awkwardly, hitting his back on the top of one of the stone fences. He grimaced with pain. He ended up on his knees and started collapsing his chute. He was disoriented and in some discomfort.

A farm boy who had been tending a flock of goats walked up. He tried to communicate with the boy.

"Can you show me the way to the coast?" Abner knew to have any hope of rescue, he had to make it to the coast where he could be picked up by an air/sea rescue boat.

The boy did not understand, and handed him a hunk of black bread, thinking he was asking for food. Across the field two German soldiers were approaching. There was nowhere to run or hide and his back was killing him.

Similar fates awaited Bonham, Thompson, and Fischler, who landed in open farm fields without incident. The last of the six crewmen to bail out was not so lucky.

Ed DeMent was heading toward the side of a mountain. Looking down he saw the ground coming up fast. As he came toward the pine trees on the mountainside, his chute caught the top of a tree. He fell through the branches, breaking each one, and landed on the rocks below dislocating both knees and hitting on his face. After laying there for a short time, he began to hurt all over. His nose was bleeding and he knew it was broken. He tried to stand up and fell back, unable to support any weight on his knees. Feeling under his flight suit, his hand came away bloody. The fall through the trees had ruptured his navel.

Both legs and arms were scraped, scratched, and bloody from the broken branches. He had landed on the side of a mountain near the city of Mostar, Yugoslavia. DeMent was in a great deal of pain, but he knew he was alive because he could hear the sound of a dog barking in the valley.

Chapter 7

The few remaining crewmen on *The Texas Ranger* were hard at work. The plane was holding steady at an altitude of 8,000 feet and flying over the Adriatic. Laszewski was flying by the seat of his pants without instruments. The drag on the plane from the damaged nose section and the feathered number two engine had reduced the airspeed to somewhere around 100 miles per hour. The plane was barely flying and was a sitting duck.

Howard Kiefer in the nose turret had been a forgotten man. The intercom was not working and he had never heard the order to bail out. Once he realized most of the crew was already out of the aircraft, the plane had begun to gain altitude again. He dropped out of the nose turret to the cabin floor where George Dancisak, the flight engineer, was attending to Milton Halberstadt, the navigator. Dancisak looked at Kiefer.

"What's your name again sergeant?" Dancisak asked.

"Howard Kiefer. How is the lieutenant?" He asked back.

"I bandaged his hand and stopped the bleeding, but he lost a lot of blood. He is still conscious. Help me get his flak jacket off and let's look at his chest," Dancisak replied.

Halberstadt moaned loudly as his flight and flak jackets were removed. Dancisak lifted his fatigue shirt to look at his injury. He felt something hard in Halberstadt's shirt pocket. There was a large and ugly contusion on his rib cage. Possibly some ribs were broken. Dancisak opened Halberstadt's shirt pocket to retrieve the object. To his surprise, it was Hal's lucky silver dollar that he carried on every mission. It had been bent almost in half by the force of the 88 millimeter fuse. George held it up so Halberstadt could see it and said,

"Hal, your lucky silver dollar just saved your life."

"I knew that dollar would come in handy one day." He replied weakly. "George, what happened to the rest of the crew?"

"Some of them had to bail out, but don't worry about that now," Dancisak said.

Halberstadt tried to sit up but didn't make it and Dancisak caught hold of him. Then he helped him back into his flight jacket. The dented flak jacket was tossed aside.

"You better just lie there Hal, you've lost a lot of blood."

The morphine was kicking in but before he was out of it he asked Dancisak to get a little closer to him so he could speak without having to yell.

"George, I wrote a compass heading down on a paper on the ledge I use for a desk. That's the heading to get us back." Hal looked up at Keifer who was now standing over him.

"Sergeant Kiefer, go up and man the top turret where you can cover the plane better. And that's an order!" Halberstadt barked weakly.

Dancisak found the piece of paper and gave it to Kiefer to take to Laszewski. When he was gone George smiled and said,

"Take it easy Hal, we have it under control."

"George, I think that was the first time I ever gave anyone a direct order," Halberstadt said.

"You sounded just like a real officer Hal, now get some rest."

When Kiefer arrived in the cockpit, Laszewski was surprised that he was still aboard.

"What are you still doing here sergeant?" He asked in a challenging tone.

"I never heard the order to bail out, sir. And now I want to move to the top turret where I can cover the aircraft better if we are attacked." Laszewski gave him a cold stare. "Sir, someone had to stay to help out. Here is a compass heading the navigator said will get us back to base."

With that, Kiefer climbed into the top turret and started rotating the dome and scanning the sky for enemy fighters. For now, the aircraft's hydraulics were still working.

Laszewski glanced at the paper Kiefer had handed him. It read "210°". He made a slight course correction to put the aircraft on the new compass heading.

Jeff Laszewski was upset. His best friend and co-pilot had bailed out over enemy territory. That action had probably saved the aircraft. If the substitute gunner had heard the command to jump and had bailed out first, Hartman would probably still be beside him helping to fly this wounded duck. Had Kiefer heard the order to bail out and ignored it? And why was Dancisak still on the aircraft?

"George, come up here for a moment." Laszewski yelled down to the nose compartment.

Dancisak crawled out of the nose and climbed up to the flight deck and into the cockpit.

"Why didn't you bail out with the rest of the crew?" Laszewski asked.

"My parachute was lost out of the bomb bay when the crew was trying to lighten the ship."

"I know, but you could have taken Halberstadt's chute, he couldn't use it." Laszewski offered.

"I thought of that, but I just couldn't leave Hal the way he was bleeding. And I wouldn't leave him to die alone in a crash." Dancisak replied.

Laszewski paused a moment before he spoke again. His voice was full of melancholy and a sense of loss.

"I never dreamed this would happen. I always knew there was a possibility of getting shot down, but I thought we would go down as a crew. I just didn't have any time to think of another way. We were losing altitude so fast."

George Dancisak put his left hand on Laszewski's right shoulder and said,

"Jeff, there wasn't anything else you could have done. There wasn't anything left to throw out and at least those guys have a chance to get back. I am just sick about losing the crew. We were really a good team." After a pause George continued, "You know, both of us will be going back to an empty tent tonight." Then he said, "I have to get back to Hal."

Laszewski nodded and then said,

"George, you know this plane as well as anyone. When we land this bird, I need you in the co-pilot seat to help with the controls. I don't know if we can get the landing gear down or not at this point."

"Just let me know when you need me." Dancisak jumped down from the flight deck and crawled back into the nose. He took off his flight jacket and used it to cover Halberstadt who was shivering noticeably. George started rooting through the first aid kit looking for another syringe. He found the morphine and injected the contents into Halberstadt's leg.

"We're gonna make it Hal, thanks to your compass heading." George said.

For a while they were both quiet. Then somewhere over the Adriatic Hal started singing,

"Oh what a Beautiful Morning . . ."

Chapter 8

The partisans who had captured Howard Hartman were pro-Nazi and turned him over to a German patrol. Hartman was blindfolded and his hands were tied behind his back. He was placed in another truck. There were others from the crew in the truck but he couldn't see them, just heard some movement. The German soldier guarding them in the back of the truck had ordered,

"No talk, talk verboten!"

So Hartman and whoever else had been placed in the truck were silent. When the truck stopped, they were helped down from the back. Hartman caught a glimpse under his blindfold of a stone farmhouse as he stepped down from the truck. He and the other men were escorted down a flight of stairs to a dark, cold room which felt like a cellar. Again they were "verboten" to speak by the soldier guarding them.

After some time passed, Hartman asked for some water. He was lead up the steps and out to a well in front of the house. Someone handed him a ladle of water. As he tilted his head back to drink, he saw Thompson, out of the bottom of his blindfold, sitting on the ground with his back leaning against the well.

"*Thompson*," Hartman whispered.

Immediately, the ladle was knocked from his hand and he was pushed back down into the cellar.

The six crewmen had bailed out at approximately 10:00 a.m. It was close to 3:30 p.m. before Ed DeMent heard voices. He had rolled into a shallow culvert and had tried to cover himself with leaves. But with his injuries, he was not able to complete the job. The voices were German. They had no trouble finding him since most of his parachute was still caught up in the tree. He was surrounded by two German soldiers with burp guns and four young Yugoslav boys with shotguns. Two of the boys picked DeMent up and carried him down the mountainside. The pain from his injuries was getting worse.

Down in the valley, he was blindfolded with his hands tied, and put into the back of a Ford truck, which was driven for some time until it came to a village. The German soldiers left DeMent unattended while they went inside a building. Soon Ed heard a lot of loud talking and yelling outside the truck. Suddenly, he was grabbed and pulled out of the truck by an angry mob of civilians. They started kicking him in his back and stomach and punching him in the face and about the head. For some reason, his wounded legs were not kicked. DeMent started screaming in agony. Had his legs been kicked he thought sure he would have died.

Finally, with all of the commotion, the guards came out of the building, firing their rifles in the air. The crowd quickly disbursed. DeMent was put back in the truck hurting all over from the beating. The truck made several stops. At each stop other crew members were picked up. Soon all six were on the truck.

The truck bounced around on gravel roads and didn't stop until after dark. The men were taken off the truck and marched into a large civilian prison. They were now in Mostar, Yugoslavia. Each of the crew was interrogated individually by a German major who spoke broken English. The men each gave their name, rank, and serial number and didn't answer any other questions.

After the last man was interrogated, they were all standing in a small room outside the major's office. Three German soldiers were guarding them and motioned for them to take off their clothes. The Germans were looking for any concealed weapons and wanted to search each man's clothes to see what else they carried with them. They stripped down to their skivvies.

When Samuel Fischler took off his fatigues, he had his pajamas on underneath. The three German soldiers and the major all broke out in thunderous laughter. All the prisoners were embarrassed. Here they were trying to be stoic and strong in front of their captors and then this. It was a real blow to their morale. In Fischler's defense, the pajamas provided an extra layer of clothing to help insulate him from the minus 40 degree temperatures during the flight. But the crew's embarrassment was complete. The men were finally allowed to get dressed again.

The major gave some orders and the crew was taken to the third floor. Because of DeMent's injuries, he was carried to a cell. Two men were assigned to a cell. They were brought food and water for the first time. The meal consisted of German black bread, meat, and ersatz coffee. Afterward, they only saw their fellow crewmen when they were taken to use the facilities.

DeMent and Thompson were put in the same cell. They were awakened at 4:30 a.m. by crying, screaming, and shouting. Edward Thompson, looking through a small opening in the cell door said,

 "They are carrying, dragging, and pulling young boys and girls down the hall. Maybe they are going to be interrogated."

That, as it turned out, was not to be the case. A short time later, DeMent and Thompson heard machine gun fire below their cell window. The wall below their cell was the execution wall. The young people were captured anti-Nazi partisans that had been rounded up the day before. Now they were dead.

"My god!" said Thompson, "They shot them all. Ed, do you think that they believe we are partisans?"

"I don't know. I am not sure whether the major believed we were Americans. The plane didn't crash. I saw it fly out over the sea. For all they know, we are just some spies that parachuted into the country." He paused and then asked, "Thompson, can you help me get my boots off. I think my feet are swollen?"

DeMent moaned as Thompson began to pull his boots off. He still was in a great deal of pain. Just then, a German soldier came into the room with some coffee on a tray. He looked at the moaning prisoner. DeMent had placed his military dog tags in his right sock before the mission. Most crewmen didn't wear their dog tags because of the extreme cold at 25,000 feet. The dog tags could actually freeze to your chest at that altitude. But DeMent just put them in his sock for safe keeping. The dog tags had fallen out of his sock when his right boot was pulled off by Thompson.

The German set the tray down and picked up the dog tags and examined them. He left the room, presumably to show them to the major. Shortly thereafter, two German guards returned and carried DeMent to the major's office. The major held DeMent's dog tags in his hand and said,

"You are from Chicago? Do you know Al Capone the Chicago gangster?"

DeMent shook his head "no".

"You are a member of a bomber crew?" The major asked.

DeMent nodded "yes".

"Are all six of you from the same bomber?" The major then asked.

DeMent said, "Yes sir."

"Then where is the plane?" The major continued.

DeMent just shrugged. The German major said,

"Then I will not shoot you. *Sergeant, for you the war is over.* You sure you don't know Al Capone?"

Again DeMent shook his head "no". The major instructed the guards to carry him back to his cell. DeMent couldn't help but smile. The Al Capone question was just too funny and his dog tags may have saved them all from the firing squad.

Within a day, Hartman was taken away. After two days confinement, a German medic rendered first aid to DeMent for his knees. He put one of DeMent's legs between his legs and with a jerk, put the kneecap back into the socket. Then he went through the same motion with the other leg. The pain was so severe that DeMent passed out. Two days later he was able to stand and walk slowly with a noticeable limp. Nothing was done for his broken nose except the blood was wiped off with a rag. A salve was put on the many cuts on his arms and legs. DeMent's ruptured naval was not looked at.

After a few days, the four enlisted men and Bonham were placed on a civilian train for Belgrade, Yugoslavia. Four guards were assigned to escort them. When the train stopped at a station, one of the guards would leave and return with a large cup of soup. The soup was just chicken or beef broth which the five prisoners had to share. The men were hungry.

"I sure would love a steak dinner about now." Thompson said.

Fred Abner began to drool. He was so hungry he could have eaten shoe leather. No one had eaten any solid food in several days. The German guards laughed loudly at the sight of Thompson making Abner drool.

The train moved slowly on its way, often having to stop and pull onto a side track as priority German military traffic passed by. The men made a game out of making Fred Abner drool at the mention of steak dinners. Finally they arrived at the main prisoner interrogation center in Belgrade.

Chapter 9

After what seemed to Jeff Laszewski to be an interminable amount of time, the coast of Italy came into view. Although Howard Kiefer had seen several enemy fighters, none had approached the crippled aircraft. Halberstadt was able to sit up with Dancisak's help and lean against the bulkhead.

"Hal, you'll be going home soon."

"Yeah, I guess my flying days are over. I can't say that I'll miss them. I just hope the guys who jumped are okay." George looked at Hal and replied,

"Yeah, we lost some good friends today. I hope they made it."

Laszewski yelled down to Dancisak,

"George, get up here and see if you can get the landing gear down."

Dancisak came up to the flight deck, grabbed Kiefer out of the top turret, and showed him how to crank one of the wing mounted landing gears down manually, while he cranked the other. The handles to crank the landing gear down were located in the damaged bomb bay. The two men had to stand on the cat walk, lean out over the opened bomb bay, and rotate the long handle clockwise for 71 turns, according to the flight manual. Both men thought it took a significant number of more turns before the landing gear locked in place. All the time, they could see the ground rushing by below them through the broken bomb bay doors.

Dancisak went back into the nose area and opened the panel to the nose gear, braced himself with his foot, grabbed the nose wheel shaft, and pulled the shaft of the nose wheel back and upward to rotate the gear into the locked position. By that time he was exhausted and out of breath. But just maybe, they would be able to land this junk heap and somehow stop it before they ran out of runway. He went up to the cockpit, sat in Hartman's co-pilot seat, and buckled up the seat belt.

"Jeff, we better fire off a flare as we come in to let them know we have a wounded man aboard," Dancisak said.

"That's right." Laszewski replied. He turned around and yelled up toward the top turret, "Sergeant Kiefer. Find the flare gun and get it connected and loaded. Fire it when we are on final approach."

Kiefer dropped down from the top turret to the flight deck. He found the flare gun in a canvas bag, reached up and inserted the barrel into the hole in the fuselage above the flight deck provided for the gun, and gave it a twist to lock it home. He then picked up a red flare from the bag, pushed it into the chamber, and closed the gun.

"Flare gun loaded and ready, sir," Kiefer informed the cockpit.

Dancisak looked over at the pilot. Laszewski's face was drawn and deep creases furrowed his forehead and sides of his eyes. He looked to be exhausted by the long hours of concentration with no co-pilot next to him to give him a break.

"What's the plan, sir?" He asked Laszewski.

"I'm going to need you to help hold the plane steady. With the nose shot up it is going to be hard to keep the plane level when we get down low and lose air speed, especially if there is a crosswind. Just help me with the control wheel, but don't fight me if I start to steer. Got it?"

Dancisak nodded and said, "Sure I got it, let's see if we can get this bird down."

S/Sgt. Bob Perry, a member of the ground crew, was working on an engine of a parked B-24, just off the south end of the runway. He wiped his forehead with a rag, and glanced down the runway toward the horizon. A plane was coming in, and he could see the number two engine was feathered. Something else didn't quite look right. The nose of the aircraft was badly damaged. "That should make it a bit dicey to fly", Perry thought. Just then a red flare burst above the plane indicating a wounded man on board.

Laszewski and Dancisak both held onto their respective control wheels tightly. The plane was trying to nose down and they had to constantly fight, by pulling back on the control wheels together, to bring the nose back up. Then it would pull down again. At the last moment, they both pulled up and the plane hit hard on its two wing-mounted landing gear. Then the plane was airborne again for about 50 feet and hit hard on the steel plated runway, this time with all three wheels making contact.

Laszewski cut the power to the remaining engines and then yelled at Dancisak,

"Hit the brakes now!"

Both men hit the brake pedals on their side of the cockpit floor. Initially, they were thrown forward against their seat belts as the brakes were applied to the wheels, but then there was nothing. The plane raced down the runway gradually slowing until it stopped just a few feet from the end.

Bob Perry had never seen a plane use that much runway to land without running off the end and crashing. When it finally stopped, he ran to the plane and popped up through the broken bomb bay to see if he could help out.

"Hey, you guys alright?" Then he noticed that no one was in the waist area or tail turret. "Where is the crew?" He yelled.

Kiefer had already jumped down from the flight deck and was walking toward the bomb bay.

"They had to bail out," was all he said.

Laszewski and Dancisak were both soaked with sweat. They looked at each other,

"Wow that was a heck of a ride, sir," Dancisak said.

Laszewski looked at his flight engineer/co-pilot and said,

"Thanks George, I couldn't have managed without your help."

Bob Perry had made his way to the flight deck.

"That was some landing. Rough mission, huh?" He asked.

Dancisak looked up at him and said,

"Not as rough as for the boys that had to jump. Listen, we have a wounded navigator in the nose. Help me get him out."

Perry and Dancisak crawled up to the nose cabin and together were able to hand Halberstadt out of the plane through the opening in the nose wheel compartment where Kiefer, standing under the plane, caught him. He was doubled over in pain and blood was soaking through the gaze wrapped around his injured hand. Because of the flare, an ambulance had been dispatched by the control tower as the plane landed. It arrived and Haberstadt was loaded into the back.

"We'll take it from here boys."

George looked into the back of the ambulance and said,

"Take it easy Hal. I'll come see you when I get the chance."

An officer drove up in a jeep. Laszewski had the cockpit window opened and yelled down,

"Hey what do you want me to do with this wreck?"

The officer told him to taxi the plane to the nearest unoccupied pad. Laszewski restarted two of the good engines as Dancisak, Kiefer, and Perry stepped back away from the plane.

"Sergeant Perry, I need you to dig around in the number two engine and find that piece of flak that busted us up," Dancisak said,

"Okay, I can do that for you," Perry nodded and said.

They watched as Laszewski taxied the plane to an open pad and cut the engines. Then he stepped out of the bomb bay and started walking toward the other airmen.

Perry continued talking, "Hey, that was some piece of flying you and your pilot just did. It looks like you are going to need a new crew. I can manage a gun. Do you think I could get on your next crew as a gunner?"

Laszewski had arrived in time to hear Perry's question.

"Are you sure you want to, after seeing this?" he quipped and pointed toward the wounded aircraft.

"Sir, after seeing the way you and your flight engineer brought that crippled bird down for a safe landing, there is no one else I would rather fly with!" Perry said.

"Thanks, Sergeant. You can go talk to the Flight Operations officer and see if he will put you with us." Laszewski said.

"Yes sir, thank you!" Perry responded.

"Don't forget that piece of flak," Dancisak reminded Perry.

Laszewski, Dancisak, and Kiefer piled into the waiting jeep which sped off toward the headquarters building briefing room, but this time for a debriefing.

Ironically, today was George Dancisak's birthday. It was only now that he remembered . . .

S-T-A-T-E-M-E-N-T

While on combat mission April 3, 1944, ship number 177, in which I was flying, received a direct/hit flak while flying at an altitude of 11000 feet. Electrical system and one engine were completely put out of commission and ship was losing altitude. Six members of the crew bailed out as it was apparent that plane would crash.

The navigator was wounded by the flak and could not manipulate his chute therefore it was necessary for the remaining crew members to aid him. While adjusting his chute the engines picked up and plane was able to continue back to the base.

Due to the fact that all remaining crew members were occupied with helping the wounded officer or flying the plane it was not noticed whether or not the crew members who bailed out landed safely.

Howard G. Kiefer

HOWARD G. KIEFER,
S/Sgt.

Statement made by S/Sgt. Howard G. Kiefer a day after the mission from Missing Aircraft Report MACR # 3708

Chapter 10

Howard Hartman had been separated from the others on the second day of captivity. He was placed on a train to Frankfurt, Germany with an armed guard. The soldier guarding Hartman gave him a small chunk of cheese and an apple to eat. The train was halted many times and had to be rerouted around damaged marshalling yards – damaged by previous allied bombing missions.

The interrogation center was in Frankfort on the Mein River. Hartman was brought into a captain's office.

"What bomb group and squadron are you assigned to?" The captain asked him. Hartman replied with his name, rank, and serial number.

"Where are you from? What state and town?" The captain asked. Again Hartman repeated his previous answer. The captain seemed to get aggravated. He said testily,

"I don't have time for you stupid Americans!" He got up from his desk, went to a bookcase on the side wall, and selected a book from the top shelf. He held the cover so Hartman could read it. To his surprise and amazement, the title printed in huge block letters on the front cover read, *456th Bomb Group*. The captain sat down, opened the book, flipped through some pages and stopped. He looked up and said,

"Your name is Howard N. Hartman. You are a 2nd Lieutenant in the 456th Bomb Group, 745th Squadron. You are a co-pilot. Your home town is Shelby, Ohio. Your parent's names are . . . here you read it." He handed the book to Hartman.

Hartman was dismayed. All his pertinent information was listed in the book. They even had an article about him from his home town newspaper. How could German intelligence be so good? How could our security be so bad? It was a revelation. He handed the book back to the captain, who said,

"You see, we have the best intelligence in the world. How do you think you can win this war now?" Hartman didn't answer. He felt betrayed and defeated.

"What kind of war are we running anyway?" Hartman thought to himself. The captain called a guard who escorted him back to a holding cell.

Chapter 11

1st Lt. Jeff Laszewski and T/Sgt. George Dancisak were ushered into Colonel Thomas W. Steed's office. Steed, who had led the mission to Budapest, had managed to return with the squadron before Laszewski and Dancisak were able to limp their plane back.

He looked them over, motioned them to take a seat, and asked,

"Lieutenant, Sergeant, are you both alright?"

They each nodded affirmatively. Laszewski went over the mission again briefly with Colonel Steed. Both he and Dancisak had been thoroughly debriefed by the debriefing officer earlier.

Colonel Steed listened to Jeff's report and asked,

"How did the plane fly prior to the flak hit?"

"Like a brand new B-24 that has never seen a combat mission," Laszewski smiled and answered.

The Colonel said with some anger in his voice,

"I knew it, that crew just refuses to go into combat. And the pilot, who does he think he's kidding, wearing those six shooters? Well, they are going to spend the rest of the war on KP duty. In fact," he continued, "I am going to have them on the chow line serving dinner to each crew as they return!"

"Including the officers?" Laszewski asked.

"Especially the officers!" Colonel Steed replied firmly.

Steed shook his head and looked kindly at the two flyers in front of him. He continued,

"Boys, I know you just had a rough mission. I know you are upset about losing your friends, and I know you are worried about your navigator. Now I want you both to take two weeks off and relax as much as possible. It will take that long to put together a replacement crew anyway. There is still a war to fight and I need you both back up in a bomber, but not for awhile."

Steed paused and then continued,

"On your way out, the duty officer will give you each a two week pass to the Isle of Capri and I want you to leave immediately." Then he looked at Laszewski and said, "Jeff, thanks for checking that plane out for me." Laszewski nodded.

Steed then completed the interview with, "Any questions?" He waited a moment but there was no reply, "Then that's all men, you're dismissed."

Dancisak and Laszewski said "Yes Sir" in unison and saluted, then walked out of the Colonel's office and picked up their passes. Once they were clear of the headquarters building, Laszewski said,

"George, let's go over and see how Hal is doing." When they got to the makeshift hospital tent, they found Halberstadt had been sedated and was asleep. They asked the doctor on duty about his condition. The doctor told them that he was stable and had been given a unit of blood. He had some cracked ribs that would hurt for awhile, but would eventually heal. His hand was so mangled, however, that he would have to have several fingers amputated. They were going to drive him down to the port of Bari as soon as he was well enough to travel.

Bari was the main port in southeastern Italy. It was a major center for ships unloading supplies for both the ground and air troops. Bari had a regular hospital that was staffed with surgeons and specialists. Halberstadt would get the best care there.

Leaving the medical tent, Laszewski and Dancisak went to the chow tent. They were both famished. They ate in silence. When they had finished their meals, Laszewski started talking,

"George, we are going to have to write letters to all of the parents of the guys that bailed out. We have a couple of weeks to rest in Capri, and then we have to get those letters out as soon as we get back. Why don't you take the enlisted men and I'll take the officers. I will have to write Bonham's and Halberstadt's wives and Hartman's mother."

"Yeah, good idea, I will have to write to all the mothers, Thompson's wife, and to DeMent's girl friend also."

Laszewski and Dancisak went and visited Halberstadt in the hospital tent again before they left on leave. Halberstadt was awake and in good spirits. He had received a V-Mail letter that day announcing his wife had given birth to a baby boy, named Hans, on February 29th, a Leap Year baby. Halberstadt was ecstatic about being able to go home, not just to a wife, but to a whole family. He told the two flyers to have a great time on Capri.

Colonel Steed came to the hospital tent several days later to present Milton Halberstadt with his Purple Heart. He brought the flak jacket Halberstadt had been wearing that day and held it up so the other men in the ward could see it. The flak jacket had a very discernable dent in the right side and the Colonel used the opportunity to say this demonstrated why you should wear a flak jacket at all times while on a mission. A photographer from *Stars and Stripes* took a picture and scribbled down Colonel Steed's words. The Colonel then had a few private words for Halberstadt. He stood next to the bed and said,

"I knew we shouldn't have been there. We flew too many missions over the same route. I 'm sorry, but now you can go home soldier. Good luck."

Halberstadt, always the artist, was thinking that it may have been much more profound than that. He was married to a Hungarian, had studied, lived, and worked with Hungarians and maybe, just maybe, the bombing of Budapest was off-limits for him. Halberstadt was transported to Bari a day before Laszewski and Dancisak returned from the Isle of Capri.

Dancisak and Laszewski each sent Halberstadt a letter that arrived the day before he shipped out. They expressed their regret for not being able to get away to visit him in Bari, and both said he was a top notch navigator and good friend. Bob Perry had come through and retrieved the 88 millimeter shell fuse from *The Texas Ranger's* number two engine and Dancisak had packed it with a scarf in a package that accompanied the two letters. The scarf was a plain, gold colored silk scarf that had a drawing of the *Boojum* dragon on it, the same one painted on the aircraft's nose. The scarf had also been signed at an earlier date by the enlisted members of the crew. The letters, flak fragment, and scarf were a touching goodbye to Italy and the war.

And Halberstadt still had his lucky silver dollar, although somewhat disfigured, to carry around in his shirt pocket.

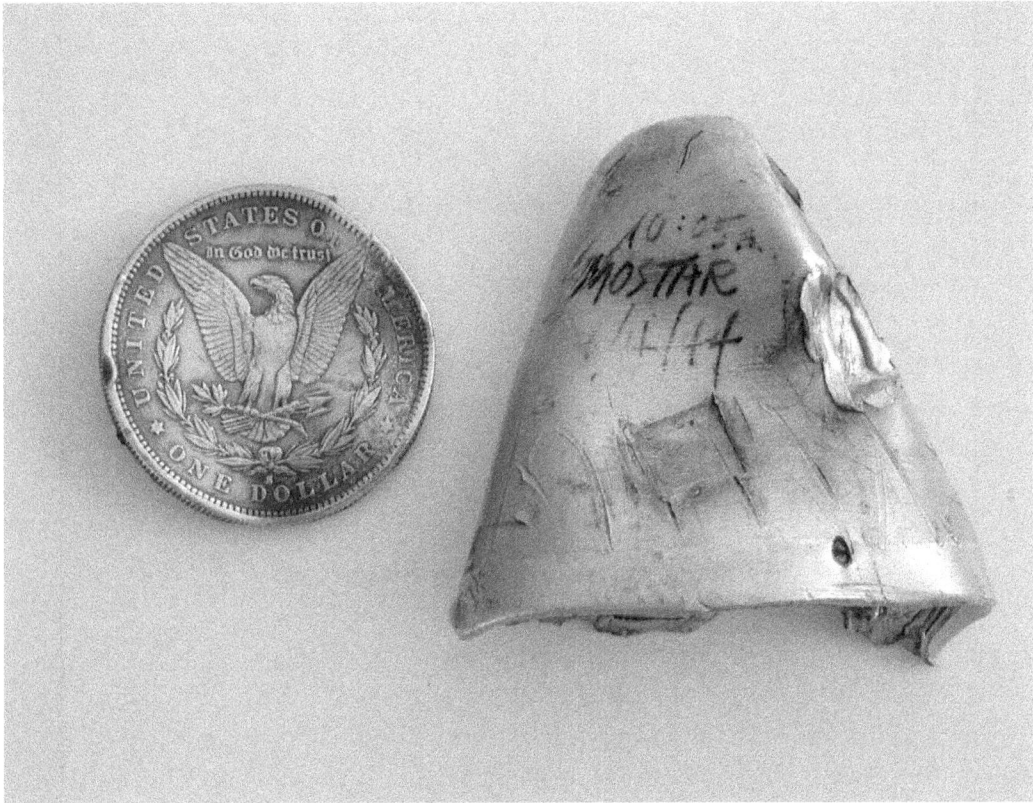

Milton Halberstadt's lucky Silver Dollar and the 88 mm Flak Fuse
Photograph provided by Hans Halberstadt

Dear "Hal:"

Excuse me for being so informal. I may not be able to get to Bari so I want to take this opportunity of telling you what a swell guy I think you are and as for a navigator you are tops. I hope that someday soon we can meet in the good old U.S.A. Maybe when you have your business in Chicago.

Loads of luck to you "Hal" and the best to the wife and little one. Don't forget to drop me a line when you get back to the States.

Sincerly

"George"

The scarf is just a small token of remembrance from Lt. Lasyewski and I.

Letter sent to Milton Halberstadt while recovering in Bari, Italy by George Dancisak
Letter provided by Hans Halberstadt

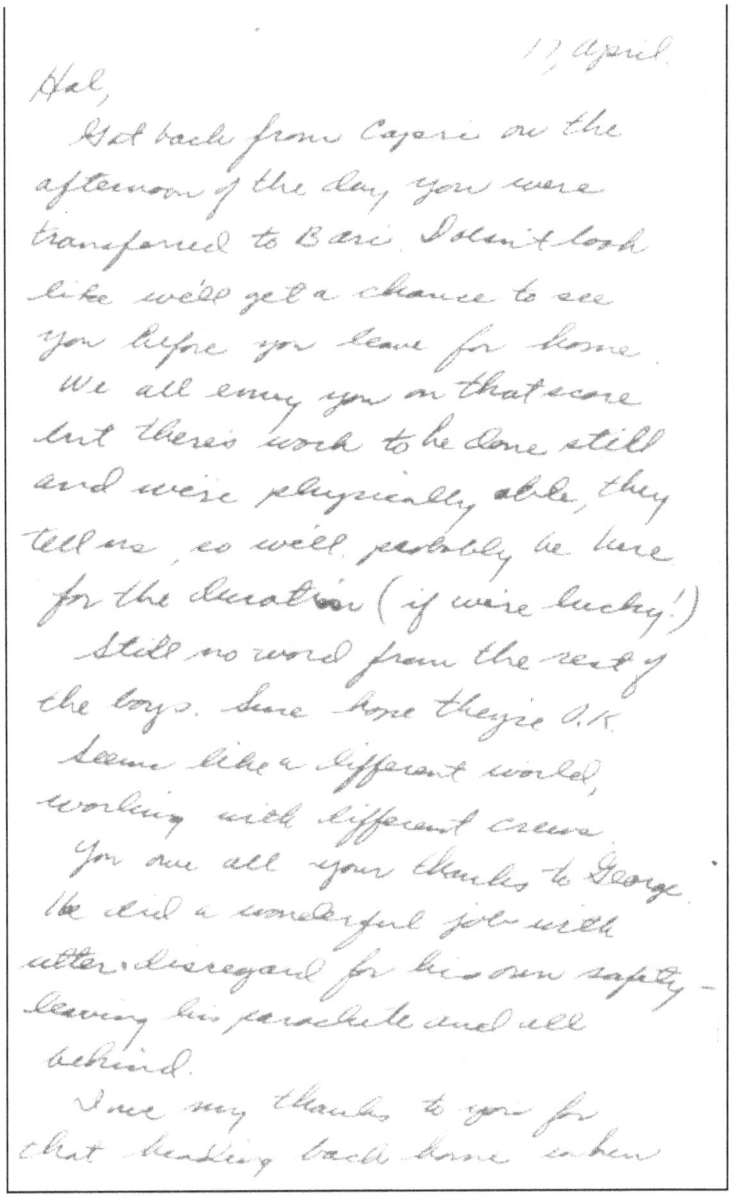

17 April

Hal,

Got back from Capri on the afternoon of the day you were transferred to Bari. Doesn't look like we'll get a chance to see you before you leave for home.

We all envy you on that score but there's work to be done still and we're physically able, they tell us, so we'll probably be here for the duration (if we're lucky!)

Still no word from the rest of the boys. Sure hope they're O.K.

Seems like a different world, working with different crews.

You owe all your thanks to George. He did a wonderful job with utter disregard for his own safety – leaving his parachute and all behind.

I owe my thanks to you for that heading back home when

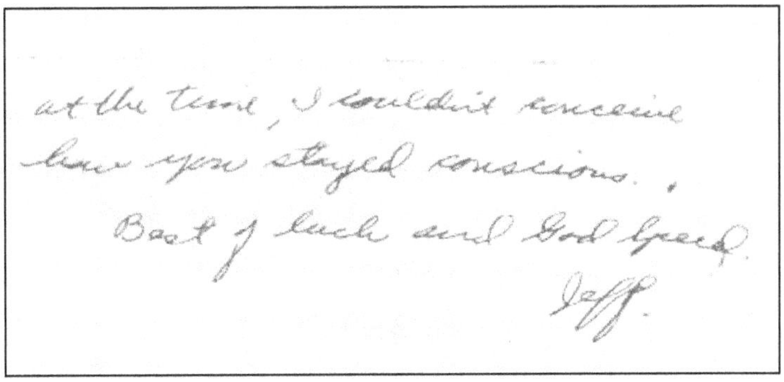

at the time, I couldn't conceive how you stayed conscious.

Best of luck and God Speed,

Jeff.

Letter to Halberstadt while in Bari sent by Jeff Laszewski
Letter provided by Hans Halberstadt

Chapter 12

After several days, the four enlisted men and Bonham were marched through the streets to a train station. The train ride took them to Stalag Luft III, about ninety miles southwest of Berlin and approximately one-half mile south of the town of Sagan, which boasted a population of about 25,000 people in the province of Silesia, not far from the Polish border.

There were five compounds at Stalag Luft III. The British were in the North and East compounds, the Americans were in the West, Center, and South compounds. Apparently, the camp had not been located there by accident. The spot was well away from all combat zones and even further away from any friendly or neutral territory. Sagan lay at the juncture of six rail lines, making it easy to transport prisoners to the camp from all over the war zone.

German Prisoner ID card and dog tags of S/Sgt. Frederick G. Abner, Jr.
Photographs provided by David F. Abner

All four of the enlisted crew members, Fred Abner, Ed DeMent, Sam Fischler, and Ed Thompson were together in the same barracks in Center compound for four weeks in

May. Then Abner and Thompson were moved to West compound. The four would meet again later at Stalag Luft VIIA. Edward Bonham was also a prisoner at Stalag Luft III but was not held in the same compound as the enlisted men.

Abner thought about his plight, about the radar jamming tinsel, about the 88 millimeter flak guns that had been moved up by the Germans on train cars right into their flight path, and wondered if the base at Stornara had been infiltrated by spies. He would never know.

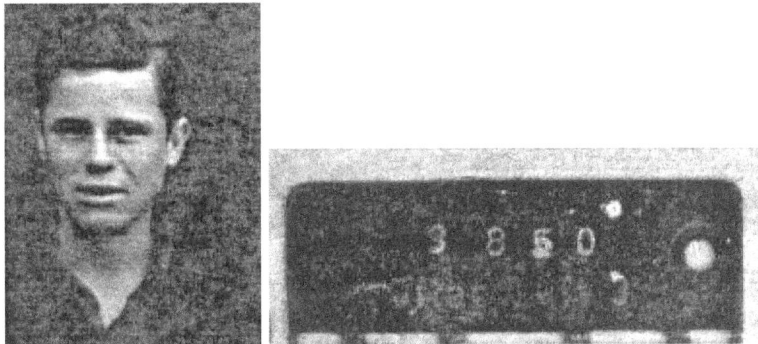

Picture from S/Sgt. Edward L. DeMent's German prisoner ID card and one dog tag.
Note the number on the dog tag is sequential with Fred Abner's.
Photographs provided by Edward L. Dement from his book
"Sargent, for you the War is Over"

The routine of life in Stalag Luft III began the moment the prisoners passed through the main gate into the *vorlager*, or main assembly area. First the prisoners were counted and thoroughly searched, finger-printed, and photographed. Then the men were issued their bedding; two blankets, one sheet, one mattress cover (that held the wood shavings for the mattress and served as a bottom sheet), one pillow case, one pillow filled with straw, and one small facial towel.

Roll Call at Stalag Luft III
Courtesy of the USAF Academy Libraries

The clothing the men were given consisted of one overcoat, three pairs of socks, a pair of wool trousers, three shirts, three pairs of winter underwear, one sweater, one pair of high shoes, a scarf, a pair of gloves, one belt or suspenders, a cap, and four handkerchiefs.

Since the clothes were provided by the Red Cross and considered a loan rather than a gift, the prisoners were told not to modify them. For cooking utensils, the prisoners were given a two-quart heavy mixing bowl, a cup, a knife, a fork, and a spoon. These items would not be replaced if lost or broken.

Center compound of Stalag Luft III consisted of 20 barracks, a cook house, theater, shower building, and laundry building. Each barracks had a central hallway with rooms on both sides. In each barracks there were 13 rooms each accommodating 12 to 16 men, a washroom, a tiny kitchen, and a latrine. Each room or cooking group was assigned a scheduled time period to cook on the communal stove. The time periods were rescheduled on a rotating basis.

Each night, German guards with their German Shepherd dogs would make the rounds at 10:00 p.m., barricading the barracks doors with a wooden bar. No one was permitted out of the barracks at this time, and another group of guards and dogs constantly patrolled the area to see the rule was observed.

Radios were not permitted in camp by the Germans, but BBC (British Broadcasting Corporation) news was carefully circulated among the men, attesting to the presence of concealed sets. One set was hidden in a British cigarette carton, measuring four inches in length, three inches high and eleven-sixteenths of an inch in thickness. When available, the news was carried from barracks to barracks by a newsman whose arrival in a pre-arranged room was announced to the barracks by the call "Soups On".

The prisoners eventually recognized various stages of *barbed-wire psychosis* in themselves and others. The mildest forms consisted of nothing more than the increasing inability to concentrate. The worst cases finally turned into insanity. Most prisoners had little difficulty recognizing the symptoms in someone else. The men did their best to cheer their comrades up when it was evident they had the blues. The reading of the underground news from the BBC also helped keep spirits up.

There were restrictions on the number of letters prisoners could receive from home. Many men waited six months to receive their first letter. Ed DeMent didn't receive his first letter until October 1944. Through these infrequent letters, the men learned their crewmates had survived and managed to get the plane back to Italy.

When given the opportunity, Fred Abner volunteered to work in the cook house, to help relieve the boredom. There, large vats of soup were prepared to supplement the prisoner's diet. The soup was mainly broth with a few vegetables, potatoes, cabbage, radishes, and maybe a carrot, and on rare occasions pork or horse meat. The main sustenance for the prisoners was provided by food parcels from the Red Cross.

Prisoner filling a Soup Vat
Courtesy of USAF Academy Libraries

Each Red Cross food parcel was a cardboard box containing four food boxes. The parcels arrived sporadically due to the uncertainty of rail travel in Germany as the war progressed. Normally, one parcel was provided for each room, or for each 12 to 16 prisoners. The parcels contained items such as Spam, canned corn beef and salmon, powdered milk, Velvetta cheese, cigarettes, Nescafe coffee, sugar, 4 ounces of chocolate, K-Ration biscuits, margarine, jam or orange preserves, and soap.

The contents of the Red Cross parcels, which were intended to feed four men, would have to be divided between the men in a room. And there was no guarantee when the next parcels would arrive and be distributed by the Germans. The German guards would often hold back the Red Cross parcels as a means of punishment. Later, the prisoners would find out the Germans actually horded the Red Cross parcels in a warehouse.

DeMent's broken nose had never been treated. He would wake up many mornings with blood on his mattress from nosebleeds while he slept. Finally he went to see one of the prisoner doctors who was British. He arranged with the German guards to have DeMent, and five other prisoners who were also suffering with various ailments that could not be treated in camp, taken to a civilian hospital. The six prisoners first had to sign a paper declaring they would not try to escape during the trip.

The men traveled by train to a small town a 100 kilometers south of Sagan that had been untouched by the war. There they went to a large and modern glass windowed hospital run by Catholic Nuns. At the hospital a German doctor cauterized DeMent's nose. After all the prisoners were treated, the German guards took the prisoners to a local *Hoffbrau* where they were allowed to drink a beer and have a ham and cheese sandwich. None of the prisoners back at Stalag Luft III ever believed that story. But to DeMent, it was one of the few good times he would experience while a prisoner of war.

For exercise, the men would walk around a perimeter road inside the prison camp fence. There were guard towers at various points along the fence and if a prisoner got too close to the fence, a guard in the tower would shoot at him. Some prisoners died because they strayed too close to the fence.

Although it is every prisoner's duty to try to escape, this had been discouraged after the escape from the British compounds, known as *The Great Escape,* resulted in the execution of 50 of the 76 escapees. *The Great Escape* had taken place in March 1944, a month prior to the crew's arrival.

No one doubted the outcome of the war. The news, especially after June 6, 1944, the date of the D-Day invasion, was mostly positive and kept hope alive for the prisoners.

The men would talk about home and what they would do when the war was finally over and they were free.

"I have a job waiting for me back in Alexandria, Virginia." Fred Abner would tell Ed Thompson. "I was an electrician's apprentice before the war and once this war is over I will go back to that job and get my electrician's license. There should be lots of work when all the GIs return. Everyone is going to need a new house."

"Well," Thompson would begin in his southern drawl, "It'll be swell to get back home again to a normal life. I'm not sure what I'm going to do but I guess there will be plenty of work for those who want it."

And so most conversations were not about the present, but about what the future would bring.

Chapter 13

Jeff Laszewski and George Dancisak had spent the two weeks since the mission of April 3rd in a state of disbelief, bewilderment, and guilt. They couldn't believe that in such a short period of time they had lost their friends and crewmen.

Both men felt a sense of guilt. Dancisak felt guilty that he was not one of the crew to bail out. He had lost his best friend, Fred Abner, as well as his tent mates Ed DeMent, Ed Thompson, and Sam Fischler. He felt that by not going out of the plane with them, he had somehow betrayed their friendship. Laszewski had similar feelings of guilt about ordering Howard Hartman to bail out. In his mind, he should have remembered Howard Kiefer, the substitute gunner, and ordered him out of the plane instead.

"I could have taken Hal's chute and jumped. Then Howard could have stayed on the plane." Dancisak would say. Laszewski would try and console Dancisak by saying,

"George, it was my ship and I decided who would jump. I only wish I had remembered about Kiefer. You did the right thing by taking care of Hal. He may not have survived if you hadn't given him first aid. No, I was the captain, and it was my decision and my fault." To that Dancisak would reply,

"Jeff, the plane was going down. You had no time, and you made the right decisions. From the time we were hit until the men bailed out, what was it, about six or seven minutes?"

Dancisak continued, not expecting an answer to his rhetorical question,

"As far as we know, everyone is alive. Would we all be alive if you hadn't decided to jump the crew? I don't think so. You did the best you could in the time you had." But Laszewski was never satisfied,

"There had to be some way to save the ship and the crew . . . now we will be thought of as jinxed and no one will want to fly with us."

"That *ground-pounder*, Bob Perry wants to fly with us."

"Well, he may be the only one, George."

Both men had traveled by truck to the port of Naples for a boat ride across the Mediterranean to Capri for their much earned two weeks leave.

Port of Naples from the boat to Capri
Photograph provided by Michael J. Dancisak

On the Isle of Capri, the two had to separate because the officer's quarters and enlisted men's quarters were in different hotels, and officers and enlisted men were not supposed to fraternize.

But they did get together again for several meals, a boat ride to see the Blue Grotto, and a cable car ride to the top of the highest mountain on Capri to take in the view. All in all it was a relaxing two weeks, except for the persistent memories of the April 3rd mission.

View from the Cable Car on Capri
Photograph provided by Michael J. Dancisak

When they returned to Stornara, they were unsure of what would happen. And their feelings were more compounded when they found out that on April 12, 1944, while in Capri, their old plane, the beloved *Boojum*, had been shot out of the sky on a mission over Austria. Now, not only did they not have a crew, but they also did not have a bomber to fly.

16 April 1944

On 12 April 1944, we were flying in formation over Bad Voslau, Austria. Our plane was the #4 ship in fox (6th) flight and Lieutenant Meyers was flying ship #292 (Boojum), in fox 3, to our left front.

Just after releasing our bombs on the target, our flight was attached by over twenty (20) enemy fighters, who made successive attacks and who closed within 100 yards. Just a few minutes later, a large shell or rocket was observed to strike Lieutenant Meyers' plane and one engine was seen to be smoking badly. Almost immediately, one other engine was seen to flame and then one entire wing was ablaze. Lieutenant Meyers' ship pulled up and away from the formation to the left and ten (10) men were seen to parachute out. All parachutes opened. Just about the time the last man was seen to parachute out, his airplane was seen to head straight down toward the target, blazing all over. It soon passed from sight.

Norman O. Grimm, 1st Lt. A. C.   Kenneth O. Couch, 2nd Lt. A. C.

Statement transcribed from microfiche file of Missing Aircraft Report MACR # 3710 describing the last moments of *Boojum*. The last sentence in the report is a fitting epitaph for the plane so named.

During the days before they had to fly again, Jeff Laszewski wrote letters home to Hartman's mother, and Bonham's mother and wife. George Dancisak wrote to Abner, Thompson, and Fischler's mothers, and DeMent's mother and girl friend. Each letter explained the circumstances of the mission and expressed the hope that the boys had survived their jump and were either trying to get back to the base, or perhaps were prisoners of war. They also cautioned that it might be some months before they knew the whereabouts of their son, husband, or boyfriend.

Finally a makeshift crew of other flyers who were without a permanent assignment was put together. Colonel Steed was good to his word about giving Laszewski a plane for the duration. The plane was the *Sky Gazer* (tail number 42-52309) and the new crew flew this plane on most missions from April 21, 1944 to mid-June 1944.

The *Sky Gazer* was shot down while being flown by another crew on June 16, 1944 over Vienna, Austria. Tragically, Howard Kiefer was killed in action that day on the *Sky Gazer*. Laszewski was then assigned to a new plane that had been flown over from the States by a replacement crew who had named it the *Reluctant Beaver*. The replacement crew was assigned to an older aircraft.

The *Reluctant Beaver*
Photograph provided by Michael J. Dancisak

Dancisak and Laszewski flew again on April 21, 1944 on a mission to Bucharest, Romania to bomb the railroad marshalling yards. The mission was a disaster. The target was heavily overcast, so no bombs were dropped. The formation was attacked by heavy flak and by sixty five enemy fighters. Four bombers were shot down. The enemy also lost four fighters, with four more probably lost, and three fighters with heavy damage.

Bob Perry had his first action manning the nose turret. Although he had shot at a lot of fighters, he couldn't tell whether he hit any or not. The experience had gotten his adrenaline pumping faster than any other experience in his lifetime. And he had lived through it all. He would never go back to being a *ground-pounder* again.

Because of all the maneuvering during the attack from the fighters, and because they had not dropped their bomb load, some aircraft were experiencing fuel shortages on the return flight.

"George, get up here." Laszewski ordered. The plane was over the Adriatic Sea headed for home.

Dancisak stood between the pilot and co-pilot and said, "Yes sir?"

"The fuel gauges are almost on empty. Are they malfunctioning, or are we about to run out of fuel?" Laszewski asked.

"Sir, with all the dodging of fighters and the payload we still have in the bomb bay, I would suspect we are running low on fuel." George replied.

"Navigator, get me to the nearest airstrip." Laszewski ordered over the intercom.

The navigator for this mission gave Laszewski a new heading for a base on the coast 30 miles north of the home base at Stornara. Laszewski managed to get the plane down just before the fuel supply ran out. Another 745th squadron B-24 piloted by Lieutenant Williamson followed the *Reluctant Beaver* into the alternate field, also due to fuel consumption problems. The planes were serviced and flew on to Stornara.

It had been another rough mission, but not as rough as the April 3rd mission.

Chapter 14

When Howard Hartman arrived at Stalag Luft 1, they had recently opened North 1 Compound, and the train load of new arrivals (arriving in box cars) were marched through the small town of Barth on the way to the camp about a mile away. The local women shouted at the prisoners and hit them with brooms and rakes as they marched past.

The prisoners were assigned 14 to a room. The room had a small cast iron stove in one corner, an oak table that could seat six on two benches, one 40 watt light bulb, and double windows which were covered at night by outside shutters. Above the windows was an opening about eight inches wide which had a cardboard cover that could be slid aside after lights were out. Guards with dogs patrolled the grounds. The men were issued one sheet, one thin blanket, and a straw filled mattress. In the winter they slept in their clothes and overcoat. It was the coldest winter in years for Barth, located on the Baltic Sea.

Red Cross parcels were issued once a week in the beginning. Several of the items were taken for the main kitchen building. It was a large building that could seat several hundred at a time. A day's food consisted of barley, with weevils in it, a little food the Germans provided, and some Spam or other canned meat from the Red Cross parcels.

Unfortunately, the mess hall burned down shortly after Hartman's arrival. After that the food was distributed directly to each prisoner. As the war progressed, the Red Cross parcels were few and far between until there were none by the spring of 1945.

As in Stalag Luft III, the men of Stalag Luft I also had a secret newspaper. The British prisoners in the compound had gotten radio parts from a guard in one of the towers who had fallen asleep. A British officer knocked on one of his legs to awaken him and told him they were going to report him to German headquarters. He offered to bring them the radio parts if they did not report him.

The British then had a radio and listened to the BBC once a day. Notes were taken on toilet paper and the Catholic priest carried them in a false pocket watch from compound to compound. Lowell Bennett, a young reporter with the International News Service who had been shot down while riding with the British on a night raid, expanded the news and published the paper know as *POW WOW - Prisoners of War Waiting on Winning*.

Hartman's bunk mate in the lower bunk, Phillip Melnick, was of Russian Jewish ancestry. He was taken, along with all other Jewish soldiers, and put in a separate barracks. They were supposed to be executed, but with the end of the war not far away, the orders were never carried out.

Hartman tried to keep his spirits up during his imprisonment, but the lack of food and harsh conditions would take its toll. Howard would lose 50 pounds during his 13 months as a POW.

Chapter 15

Flying Over the Alps
Photograph provided by Michael J. Dancisak

Jeff Laszewski and George Dancisak continued to fly missions through the months of May, June, and July. These included four missions to the infamous Ploesti, Romania to destroy Hitler's main source of oil. During the mission of May 5, 1944, George Dancisak, who was a photographer as well as flight engineer, captured on film one of the most tragic events of the war.

A B-24 flown by 1st Lt. Albert M. Lehner was badly damaged by flak and was on fire. Waist gunner, S/Sgt. Bill P. Garcia bailed out of Lt. Lehner's plane. As he fell, and before he could open his parachute, Garcia's body hit the wingtip of a B-24 flown by 1st Lt. Lawrence E. Peterson, breaking the wingtip off just beyond the number four engine. Peterson's plane immediately went into a flat spin, the number four engine fell off, and the plane went out of control and crashed. Garcia, Peterson, and all but two members of Peterson's crew were killed.

Lt. Peterson's B-24 moments after losing a wingtip
Photograph provided by Michael J. Dancisak

Dancisak happened to be taking pictures of the bomb run at the time through the camera port mounted aft of the ball turret and caught the image of Peterson's plane on its back with the wingtip gone. It was another of those sobering events that eats at the mind. Dancisak reacted to the scene in the view finder,

"Oh my God, did you guys see that?" A couple of "yeahs" were heard on the intercom.

"There but for the grace of God . . . ", Dancisak muttered under his breath.

"Okay, think about it later, we have a job to do." Laszewski ordered.

T/Sgt. George L. Dancisak, the Flight Engineer and crew Photographer
Photograph provided by Michael J. Dancisak

The rest of the mission was without incident to Laszewski's crew. At this point in the war, friendly fighters, mostly P-51's, some of which were flown by the Tuskegee Airmen, escorted the bombers on their missions. Enemy fighter activity against the bomber formations was curtailed by the escorts, and the main danger to the bomber crews was from flak.

P-51 Mustangs Flying Escort
Photograph provided by Michael J. Dancisak

On a mission to Montpellier, France, on May 27, 1944, Bob Perry, riding in the nose turret, was scanning to his left, or port side of the plane. He saw a cylinder detach from the number one engine. He didn't know if it was a fighter or flak that caused it, but the cylinder just popped straight up and then drifted back as the plane left it behind.

In the cockpit, Laszewski, who was flying with co-pilot 1st Lt. Oran R. Key, Jr., immediately feathered the prop on engine number one.

Dancisak climbed up to the flight deck to see what was going on as the plane had slowed and dropped out of formation. The plane was losing altitude at a steady pace.

"Remind you of another time, George?" Laszewski asked over his shoulder as he gripped the control wheel.

"Yep, except for what engine is out." Dancisak replied.

"I guess you guys know this drill." Lt. Keys said.

"Yeah, George and I are experts." Over the intercom Laszewski ordered, "Bombardier, salvo the bombs now." After that order was carried out, Laszewski voice came back over the intercom, "Okay crew, we have lost an engine and we need to lighten the ship. Throw everything out you can get rid of except yourselves." After a brief pause he continued, "Navigator, give me a heading to the nearest friendly air field that can handle this bird."

Then Laszewski looked back at George and said, "That about cover it Sergeant Dancisak?"

Dancisak laughed and said, "Yes sir. But maybe this time we won't have to jump. If we do, I am going first."

The navigator gave Laszewski a heading for the island of Corsica. The crew jettisoned about everything that could be detached, and the plane managed to limp into Ajaccio, Corsica. After a couple days in Corsica for repairs, the crew flew back to Stornara. On the trip home, George Dancisak took a picture of the erupting Mount Vesuvius.

Mount Vesuvius
Photograph provided by Michael J. Dancisak

Life at Stornara was not without some entertainment. Bob Hope and Francis Langford arrived with a band and the rest of their USO show to entertain the troops. Dancisak made sure he got some good pictures of the lovely Miss Langford during her performance.

Bob Hope Show with Francis Langford on stage, June 1944
Photograph provided by Michael J. Dancisak

Francis Langford entertaining the troops at Stornara
Photograph provided by Michael J. Dancisak

Dancisak was able to take a few days leave in early July. He used the time to hop a ride to Rome where he toured the city and visited St. Peter's Basilica. There he stood in a large crowd and saw and heard the Pope Pius XII speak. It was one of the highlights of his tour of duty in Italy.

The Laszewski crew flew three more missions to Ploesti; on May 18th, May 31st, and for their last mission (where else but Ploesti) on July 16th. By the end of that mission, all of Hitler's black gold in Ploesti had been completely destroyed. When the *Reluctant Beaver* finally came to rest on the parking pad at Stornara and the crew had exited the plane, George Dancisak locked the bomb bay doors for the last time. He walked away from the plane and never looked back.

In early August 1944, now Captain Emil S. (Jeff) Laszewski and T/Sgt. George L. Dancisak departed from the port of Bari, Italy on their way home. Together they had flown 50 credited combat missions and had survived three emergency landings. They considered themselves among the lucky ones having completed more then their share of missions without being killed, wounded, or captured. They were heroes, but neither man considered himself one.

The heroes were those that hadn't come back, and six crewmen of the *Boojum* who they now knew were prisoners of war.

Chapter 16

For Howard Hartman and the rest of the prisoners in Stalag Luft I, the war in Europe became a race between the British, American, and Russian armies to see who could get to Berlin first. In late April of 1945, it became evident the Russians would get to the town of Barth on the Baltic Sea where Stalag Luft I was located before the other advancing armies.

The prisoners had heard the sound of artillery pounding the German lines for the past several weeks and their expectations for freedom were high. The German commandant tried to force the American commander, Colonel Hub Zemke, to assemble his men so they could be marched out of camp to another prison camp away from the advancing Russians. Colonel Zemke refused and said his men would fight the Germans if they tried to force them to march.

On the morning of May 1, 1945, the now ex-prisoners woke up to find the German guards where gone and had been replaced by prisoner guards. The Russians arrived the next day. The Russians and the American and British prisoners celebrated and fraternized. The Russians held the camp for two weeks while they compiled information on all 10,000 prisoners.

With their newfound freedom, many of the men decided to see the countryside surrounding the prison camp. Some ex-prisoners commandeered bicycles from German civilians and toured the town of Barth or went down to the shore of the North Sea nearby. Others enjoyed walking around outside the camp. The Russians were pretty brutal in their treatment of the local German population, so many German civilian families were more then happy to take in American and British ex-POW's as houseguests. In that way, they hoped to avoid the looting taking place by the rampaging Russian army.

Meanwhile, the 8th Army Air Force in England made plans to transport the liberated prisoners to France. B-17 aircraft were stripped of armament and the bomb bays were boarded up to make floors on which to sit the prisoners. It was determined that 32 prisoners could be transported by each plane. B-17 bombers from the 91st and 389th Bomb Groups took part in the evacuation.

The now former POWs were flown out of Barth airport to Laon, France and then put on a train to Camp Lucky Strike, near Le Havre. Howard Hartman was more then happy to drink the milkshakes they were offered three times a day to fatten up. There were over 50,000 liberated prisoners at Camp Lucky Strike, waiting their turn to be ordered onto a Liberty Ship bound for New York City, and home.

Chapter 17

The men in Stalag Luft III, as well as in the other prison camps, were listening to their hidden radios and also following the progress of the allied armies. At 3:00 p.m. on January 17, 1945 the German news broadcast announced unprecedented Russian advances toward the town of Sagan where Stalag Luft III was located.

On January 22, 1945, General Vanaman, the highest ranking prisoner, and thus camp commander, ordered every compound commander to prepare the camp for possible evacuation. On January 27, 1945 at 8:30 a.m., as many men as possible crowded into the auditorium to hear what General Vanaman had to report. He told the group that one of three things was going to happen; the German guards will either evacuate or surrender the camp to the Russians, the Commandant will be ordered by some high fanatical official in Berlin to put us to death, in which event we will fight for our lives, or we will be evacuated on a long march across Germany. The Russians had advanced to within 22 miles of the camp.

In the early afternoon of Saturday, January 28, 1945, the rumble of artillery was heard approximately 15 miles away. At 9:30 p.m., the order to evacuate the camp was announced. The prisoners were told to be ready to start marching in one hour.

In the West compound, Fred Abner and Edward Thompson started packing whatever they could carry into makeshift packs made from sheets and pillow cases.

"Freddie, they must really be really desperate to want to take us out of here," Thompson said.

"Yeah, the end must be near. At least they haven't shot us yet!" Abner replied.

"Not yet, but this is going to be a real bitch, marching in the snow and sub zero temperatures. It might be better if they did shoot us!" Thompson joked.

"Just keep thinking about getting home and we'll make it." Abner said hopefully.

Ed DeMent and Samuel Fischler, in Center compound, were also getting ready for the march. The prisoners raided the supply building where the Germans had been storing the Red Cross parcels that they rationed out to the prisoners.

"Take whatever you can carry Sam." DeMent said as they waited in line to grab some rations.

"I am going to fill every pocket I can with canned food." Fischler replied.

In spite of the men's best efforts, a great deal of food was left behind. An estimated 25,000 Red Cross parcels were left, attesting to the fact the Germans had been hording the parcels instead of distributing them to the prisoners. Center compound fell out to form up for the march at 10:00 p.m. on January 28, 1945.

Everyone was warned that all guards were heavily armed and had been ordered to shoot any man who breaks rank or who deliberately disobeyed orders. For every 60 men, there was one guard and one dog on each side of the column. The dogs would prove to be more effective than the guards at keeping the prisoners in line.

Approximately 500 prisoners were too sick to be moved and were left behind with a few medical personnel, clergymen, and several healthy prisoners to help care for them.

Snow had begun to fall several days before the march began and about six inches had accumulated by the time the men left the camp. Many prisoners were able to build sleds upon which to carry their possessions. Temperatures ranged between 10 to 20 degrees below zero. Snow fell through the night and the wind created blizzard conditions at times. The harsh weather soon took its toll upon the weakened men and the columns began to stretch out as the fatigued men started to fall farther and farther behind the lead column.

While some prisoners witnessed isolated shootings, there were few such instances. However, a sergeant in front of DeMent bent down to tie his shoe. The German guard on that side of the column pulled out his pistol and shot the man in the back of the head. DeMent knelt down to help his fallen comrade. The guard shoved him away.

"He was just tying his shoe!" DeMent yelled at the guard. The guard motioned with his pistol for him to continue walking. No one was allowed to touch the dead sergeant and the guard pulled his body out of the formation and threw it into a snow bank. Of all the deaths DeMent had witnessed, this was the most senseless. After surviving all the hardships of prison camp, to be killed while tying your shoe when the war was practically over was such a shame, and in DeMent's mind it was a war crime.

The weather was cold and snow had fallen to a depth of approximately two feet, and continued to fall. German civilians were ordered to clear the center of the road as the formation passed by them through the town of Sagan. The prisoners watched in silence as soldiers of the German army and SS hurried the civilians in between the endless line of marchers to shovel snow. German civilians who resisted were shot. The SS never argued. A rifle shot saved time and settled all arguments.

It soon became clear the Germans had not made any plans for care of the prisoners during the journey. A few wagonloads of bread were sent along with several of the columns, but the prisoners ate mostly the food they carried on their backs. Prisoners bartered with civilians for some food along the way. Water was obtained by picking up snow and letting it melt in your mouth. Shortly after 8:00 a.m., the Germans ordered a 15 minute rest.

Prisoners resting during the March
Courtesy of the USAF Academy Libraries

Just past 4:00 p.m. the prisoners entered the small town of Wharton and stopped for a break. General Vanaman refused to go further without an overnight stop. He and the Commandant had a furious argument. General Vanaman stood firm and the commandant finally ordered a stop for the night.

DeMent was assigned to a Roman Catholic Church capable of seating 400 people. It took 1 hour and 40 minutes to pack 2,000 prisoners into the small church interior. The prisoners who couldn't fit into the church were left outside. There were no latrine facilities, only a small washroom. The men had to use the cemetery to relieve themselves by sitting on the tombstones.

"This is going to be a terrible sight after the snow melts in the spring," DeMent thought.

The march continued for nine more days, with the prisoners housed at night in whatever church or barn was available.

On Tuesday morning, February 7, 1945, it was announced that several freight trains would take the prisoners from Spremberg to Stalag Luft VII-A, and the trip would take three days and nights. Two trains of boxcars were pulled up on the track in Spremberg.

Fifty men were marched to, and loaded into, each boxcar. Most of the cars had been used for hauling cattle. The insides of the cattle cars were filthy. The smell was unbearable. There was no room for anyone to lie down, or even sit down. Four pasteboard boxes were placed in each of the four corners of the boxcar to be used for toilets or sickness. The prisoners suffered most from thirst. Finally, the toilet boxes overflowed.

Thursday morning the trains pulled into Regensburg. The doors opened and the men were unloaded. There was a pond just ahead of the train's engine. The prisoners broke ranks *en masse*. Guards fired rifles into the air. Nonetheless, the men moved to the water, drank, and filled cans and jars. At no time were the prisoners given food while they were on the trains.

At this point the trains were split up. Abner and Thompson on one train went to Nuremberg. DeMent and Fischler on the other went directly to Moosburg. During the trip an unfortunate incident occurred. Allied fighters, mistakenly thinking the train was carrying German troops, strafed the train killing several prisoners.

The following morning the prisoners were unloaded on the north side of Moosburg where Stalag Luft VII-A was located. It was Friday, February 10, 1945, 11:00 a.m. The ordeal had come to an end. The march had crossed a large part of Germany, a distance of 480 miles.

Route of the March from Stalag Luft III to Stalag Luft VIIA in Moosburg
Courtesy of the USAF Academy Libraries

Over 3,000 men were sick with infected stomachs, dysentery, colds, and pneumonia. All the prisoners were weak from malnutrition, mental, and physical exhaustion. DeMent's injured knees had given out after the first few days. He would be forever grateful to the men who helped support him for much of the march. He was just thankful to be alive. Samuel Fischler was also grateful that he was still alive and the long march was finally over.

Abner and Thompson had also survived the long ordeal. They were imprisoned in Nuremberg for several weeks and didn't arrive at Stalag Luft VII-A in Moosburg until early March. At that time they met up again with DeMent and Fischler.

No one was pleased to be in Stalag Luft VII-A. The overcrowding was unbelievable. Men had to sleep on floors and in tents outside the barracks. Food was severely rationed. The situation was close to intolerable.

Photographs show overcrowding at Stalag Luft VII-A

Chapter 18

In late April, a special news bulletin said that General George S. Patton and his 3rd Army were nine miles from Moosburg. General Patton dispatched a staff car under a white flag to Moosburg late in the afternoon. He asked that the Commandant, the Senior American POW, and his Chief of Staff meet at noon the next day at post headquarters at Moosburg. On April 28, 1945 at 8:00 p.m., General Patton's proposal was read requesting the Commandant surrender the Moosburg prison camp without combat. In return, General Patton guaranteed the Commandant, his staff, and all German military personnel would not be subjected to military trials for war crimes. All German personnel would be treated as POWs according to the terms of the Geneva Convention.

A Colonel in the SS was present. At his insistence, the Commandant declined the terms and decided to make a last-ditch effort to fight. The Commandant was informed that Patton's 3rd Army was part of the American 7th Army which would attack at 8:00 a.m. on April 29, 1945. Patton warned that if any of the prisoners were harmed by the Germans, those Germans would be executed.

At 8:14 a.m. large clouds of dust rolled over a hill about two miles away from the camp. Tanks, as far as the prisoners could see, were rolling down the hillside. Five squadrons of fighter planes were also flying overhead. The siren sounded loud and clear and was heard all over the camp. In a few minutes, the German guards locked the prisoners in the barracks and closed all shutters. The prisoners quickly ripped up floor boards. Men got under tables and beds. Some men laid on the floor and others under the building.

Machine gun bullets began bursting in every direction, attacking the sentry towers. The sound of tanks grew louder and the German guards started shooting back with their machine guns. The roar of tanks, planes, and guns blasted against the prisoner's eardrums. They heard the crashing and ripping of steel. Suddenly, everything stopped, except the movement of tanks close by. Out of nowhere came a Piper Cub flying low over the camp and dipping its wings, signifying the battle was over.

When DeMent got out of the barracks, there were men climbing out of windows and up to the roof. There was an American tank going through the main gate. The battle had lasted about 20 minutes. The guards that were still in the camp surrendered to the prisoner officers. The prisoners rejoiced in their new freedom.

Outside the prison camp in the town of Moosburg the prisoners could see an American flag being raised. When it unfurled at the top of the flag pole, it was flying upside down.

As DeMent looked on with several other prisoners, the flag was brought down and raised again, this time the Stars and Stripes were flying proud.

Sometime later, General Patton arrived in his command car. It was not the drab green olive color usually seen at the front, but brightly shined and suitably decorated with sirens, a spotlight, and a four-star flag.

General George S. Patton arriving at Stalag Luft VIIA, Moosburg, Germany
Courtesy of the USAF Academy Libraries

General Patton took a tour of a few buildings. Fred Abner was in the kitchen building peeling potatoes for the soup vat. He had been locked in when the Germans had shut all the prisoners up in the buildings. He had listened to the battle, heard the gunfire stop, and went back to the job at hand, sitting down and peeling potatoes. After a while, he noticed a pair of highly polished combat boots standing in front of him. He looked up and there was General Patton who said, "Son, get up, you are free!"

After his inspection of the buildings, General Patton mounted the hood of his jeep to speak. As usual, Patton was immaculately dressed in whipcord trousers, boots, battle jacket, two ivory handled pistols, and a helmet polished to a high sheen. Patton was a very imposing figure with a harsh face. He stood rigidly at attention, a man more than six feet tall, weighing approximately 200 pounds. The General grabbed the microphone which was attached to a loudspeaker on his car and addressed the crowd in a high-pitched, almost falsetto voice.

After holding up his hand for silence, General Patton looked up and saw a Nazi flag still flying. Pointing toward it, he said,

"I want that son-of-a-bitch cut down and the man who cuts it down, I want him to wipe his ass with it." Then he said,

"Well, I guess all you sons-a-bitches are glad to see me." Immediately a great roar went up. After the noise calmed down, Patton continued,

"I'd like to stay with you awhile, but I have a date with a woman in Munich. It is 40 kilometers away and I've got to fight every damned inch of the way. God Bless you and thank you for what you have done." He stepped back into his jeep and drove away.

Within an hour, three truckloads of nurses and American Red Cross workers arrived. They handed out gum, cigarettes, doughnuts, and coffee. White bread was also issued and to the men of the camp, it tasted like cake. A sound truck with a loudspeaker started playing records. The first American song the men heard was *Don't Fence Me In*.

After several weeks, the men were finally transported by C-47 aircraft to Camp Lucky Strike to await a Liberty Ship home.

Howard Hartman had already been at Camp Lucky Strike for a couple of days. One day as he was walking down the road that led from the main gate to the bivouac area, a truck drove past and a man yelled and jumped out of the back of the truck.

"Lieutenant Hartman!" As the soldier ran up to him, Hartman recognized Samuel Fischler.

"Well I'll be damned if it's not Sergeant *Static Chaser*! Hello Sam, how are you doing?" Hartman exclaimed. (*Static Chaser* was the nickname the crew had given Fischler because he was the radio operator).

"I am doing great sir, and you don't look so bad yourself." Fischler replied.

"Tell me Sam, did the other men make it?" Hartman asked.

"Yes, they are all fine, and they are all here in camp." Fischler said. Hartman felt elated. It was as if a giant weight had just been lifted from his shoulders. After all, he had been the one who had ordered the rest of the men to bail out. It was great news to hear they had all survived the war.

"Sam, let me buy you a milkshake." Hartman said.

"Yes sir, that's an order I will gladly follow!"

Fischler and Hartman turned and continued walking back toward the camp.

The six men who bailed out over Mostar, Yugoslavia on April 3, 1944 would all eventually reach home by way of crowded Liberty Ships that docked in New York City. The sight of the Statue of Liberty brought cheers and tears to the men lining the railing of the decks. After 13 months of captivity, deprivation and starvation, the remaining crewmen of the *Boojum* were finally coming home. From New York City, the men boarded trains bound for their hometowns and a 60 day leave.

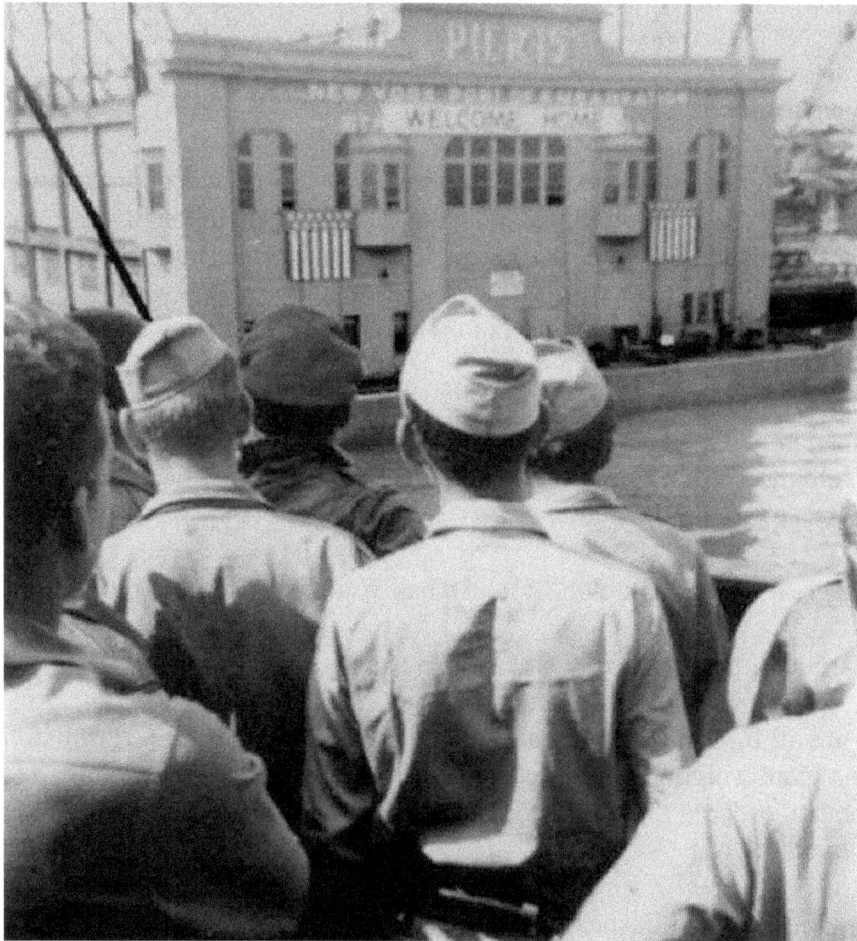

Arriving from France on Liberty Ship
Photograph provided by the 456th Bomb Group Association

When Howard Hartman stepped off the train in his hometown of Shelby, Ohio, it was late night and the station platform was shrouded in darkness. A few street lights illuminated small circles on the platform directly underneath. From somewhere in the shadows, Jeff Laszewski stepped out to greet him. The two men shook hands and embraced. Hartman would never forget the thoughtfulness of that gesture on the part of his pilot.

When Fred Abner returned home to Alexandria, Virginia, he received a call from his friend George Dancisak. The two men would never meet again face to face but would exchange telephone calls during future Christmas holidays. Dancisak would also stay in contact through the years with Howard Hartman and Milton Halberstadt. The bond forged by the incident over Mostar was reaffirmed by a phone call between Halberstadt and Dancisak every April 3rd from 1945 until 1987 when Dancisak died at the age of 70. Halberstadt continued to call George's widow every April 3rd until his death in 2000.

Ed DeMent would meet up again with Fred Abner and Edward Thompson at an air base in Miami, Florida, after the men had completed their leaves and before they were discharged from active duty. DeMent would correspond with Abner, Dancisak, and Hartman occasionally over the years.

A day before Ed DeMent was to be married in Chicago to the sweetheart he had finally gotten back to, Jeff Laszewski stopped by to wish him well. He apologized for ordering Ed and the rest of the crew to bail out. Ed told him that there was no reason to apologize because he had not had enough time to make any other decision. DeMent told Laszewski he had never questioned the decision to bail out.

Howard Hartman and Milton Halberstadt would also keep up a correspondence, and meet each other once more when Halberstadt, who had settled near San Francisco, was on a business trip to the East coast. Samuel Fischler, Edward Thompson, and Edward Bonham would each go back home and resume their previous lives. The rest of the crew would never hear from them again.

In 1948, the 747th Squadron of the 456th Bomb Group would form the 456th Bomb Group Association and have their first reunion in Chicago, Illinois. Eventually, the 744th, 745th, and 746th Squadrons would become part of the association. Ed DeMent and Howard Hartman would meet again at several of the 456th Bomb Group Association reunions. Hartman would serve terms as both Vice President and then President of the association. DeMent would become the Vice Commander and later Commander of the Florida P.O.W. Association and later become an officer in the National P.O.W. Association.

The crew of the B-24H Heavy Bomber *Boojum* returned to civilian life, married, raised families, led productive lives, retired and watched their grandchildren grow. But they would never forget their experiences during those tumultuous, war-torn years of 1943 to 1945. George Dancisak would carry the reminder of one mission physically for the rest of his life. The fuel leak that he stopped to save the plane during the mission of March 22, 1944 would leave his chest scarred and sensitive to the touch as long as he lived. Ed

DeMent would suffer from pain in his knees and walk with a slight limp from his ill-fated parachute landing on April 3, 1944.

Fred Abner would build B-24 model airplanes for his kids and later his grandchildren, reliving those days quietly as he worked on each model. Several plastic or wood B-24 model airplanes were always hanging from the back porch ceiling, and on several weekends a year, he might be found sitting at the kitchen table constructing a new B-24 model aircraft.

DeMent wrote a book entitled, *Sargent, for you the War is Over*, detailing life in Stalag Luft III, the death march in January/February 1945, and the liberation of Stalag Luft VII-A by General Patton. The chapters about Stalag Luft III and the death march are taken from Mr. DeMent's book. Howard Hartman also wrote down his prison camp experiences, after a professor at Ohio State University suggested that he could exorcise the demons that were keeping him from sleeping at night by so doing.

Few letters exchanged between these crewmen ever failed to mention the events of April 3, 1944. In 1989, Fred Abner and Ed DeMent exchanged letters reliving the events of that day. Likewise, Milton Halberstadt and Howard Hartman also exchanged letters about the mission as late as 1998.

Were these men heroes? Certainly Reinaldo C. Garza who died while flying as a replacement gunner on another B-24 during the mission of March 19, 1944 was a hero, as was Howard G. Kiefer who died on the mission of June 16, 1944. Milton Halberstadt, wounded and an amputee, certainly was heroic. Jeff Laszewski and George Dancisak completed 50 missions over enemy territory and surely must be considered war heroes. As for the men who bailed out over Mostar, Yugoslavia and subsequently spent 13 months in captivity, who would argue their heroism. So yes, these men were heroes. But none of them would ever admit to being one. To the men of the *Boojum*, there was a job that had to be done, and they did that job exceedingly well.

Crew of the B-24H Heavy Bomber *Boojum*

Frederick G. Abner, Jr.

Edward C. Bonham

George L. Dancisak

Edward L. DeMent

Samuel Fischler

Reinaldo C. Garza

Milton H. Halberstadt

Howard N. Hartman

Emil S. (Jeff) Laszewski

Edward O. Thompson

Below is a letter from **Milton H. Halberstadt** to **Howard N. Hartman** describing the events of April 3, 1944 from which much of this book's plot was developed.

Dear Howard: *January 17th,*
1990

Your Letter was in Friday's mail. It was fat enough to portend of its importance so I saved it until last to savor it – and sure enough it was more than I could handle. I read your letter written on your darting young typing machine – about your writing, while you were in college, about our 10th mission. I started to read it but could only get to the first line or two and had to set it aside until the next morning.

After the morning's coffee (a full-bodied Mocha-Java blend) to help me overcome the tension of the moment. I read your recounting of your share of the experience and the trauma when the plane we were assigned for this mission in place of our "Boojum", was hit by the fuse* of an 88mm shell over Mostar, Yugoslavia some 45 years ago. (After bouncing off my flak-suit it knocked the electrical system out and went on to lodge in the oil line of the #2 engine which had to be feathered – whew, no wonder my stomach was so sore for a week!) *Photo copies enclosed. Of the fuse – not my stomach!!

And even with the Mocha Java I still could not read straight through your saga! It took me at least 3 passes - Wow!! Little did I know! Talk about the tail of the dog – the tail of the plane! I had no idea of what you guys and the plane had gone through!

Well you talk of intuition or lack of it – I must confess that I had a premonition and for the first time in our 10 missions I plotted back-headings for this one. I firmly believed that in "combat it's always the other guy." (How else could one get through the hell of combat?) And, if I recall, I remembered it through a Morphine-laden brain – thanks, again George!, - sending it up to Jeff – by way of George, I guess. (Could it have been 210°?) But from your letter you evidently had already set the magnetic compass for the return to our base.

You of course were right: it was our 10th mission. I will send you a copy of my 1944 calendar even thought it doesn't have missions #9 and #10.

By the way, we weren't flying "Boojum" that day. ("Boojum", in case you don't remember, was the name I suggested. It's from Lewis Carroll's "The Hunting of the Snark" and "Boojum" is a mythical monster that evaporates anyone who sees it!) We were on the Great! Texan's plane, "Texas Ranger" - I blocked his name a long time ago. He's the one who wore 6-shooters on his hips; whose father drove up from Texas to the field at Kansas City (?) (what gas shortage?), our 1st nite's stop on the supposedly "Classified" start of the trip to our ultimate goal, our field in Italy. He was a month late arriving in Italy (I have never been able to watch "Catch 22" – the little I've seen of it reminds me of him and the 745th); he's the one that had never made a mission in 9 starts, and ol' reliable Jeff was chosen to prove that the plane was OK but that Tex was not. (We all were afraid – I tell everyone that "I invented brown underwear" which is almost always good for a laugh – Boy! How much easier it is to laugh about it now!)

But I digress: I was just writing in my Log: "10:05. Mostar. 10,000 feet, climbing" and I can still see the hole opening up in the fuselage just above Bonham and to the right of Keifer*, the substitute nose-turret gunner. (Amazing how the brain can at times actually slow-motion the action!) *I didn't remember it either and only found it in the Plainfield newspaper which is enclosed – with my corrections. But! I thought I had only had the breath knocked out of me and that I had only been out for maybe a minute or so!!!!! And when you told me back in Annapolis that we had gone out over the water and then came back! To let you guys parachute over land!! I was amazed!!!! I had never known this!

I remember being told we might have to ditch and I said "Go ahead." I guess that maybe that kinda made Jeff's mind up? I actually must have been out for quite a while but I remember George giving me a shot of Morphine and telling him to take the Silver Dollar that was sitting in the middle of my leg. (See newspaper clipping & photos of the Dollar enclosed)

Obviously, I must have known that some of you had jumped. I remember telling the nose-turret to take the top-turret where he could cover more – I hoped. That was the 1ˢᵗ & last time I ever used the expression: "That's an order!"

I remember singing "Oh what a Beautiful Morning!" somewhere over the Adriatic. (George gave good shots!) I realized that I was all through and that I would be going home. (I didn't know it – not to a wife but to a family – the waiting V-Mail told me that I had a son (Hans) born on Leap Year Day! Someone's always taking advantage of me: Feb 29ᵗʰ!!)

I remember telling someone that I would stay in the nose for the landing. It must have been perfect!

I remember Badami (the Sq Medic, a DC – that's right: a Colonic Doctor from San Jose, CA) saying they were going to have to cut my parachute harness to get it off. I can't recall what I said but it probably was:"*#@@%%***!!!*&&&!"

I remember a photo of someone holding up my flak-suit as an example of why one should wear a flak-suit. Though I didn't see it there was another photo of the interior of the Nav's compartment before they cleaned it up. From what I had heard it really was a mess! and I can easily sympathize with Bonham's queasiness!

I often wondered what would have happened if the plane we were substitute crew for had removed its Loran as it was ordered to do. Thank the Texan! – every other plane had removed theirs! And if I had sat in my usual place on the right of the Navigator's table where there was no Loran I think that either your or Jeff would have been, shall we say, shorter ... the trajectory was almost flat out! Draw a line from the right of the nose-

turret, through my hand to my black-and-blue stomach under my flak-suit and figure who I sat in front of ...

And I remember Col Steed giving me the Purple Heart the next day (I'm no longer sure what day it really was) and his saying; "I'm sorry. I knew we shouldn't have been there." I like to think it may have been more profound than that – I married a Hungarian; studied and lived and worked with Hungarians and maybe, just maybe – that bombing Budapest was off-limits for me.

That's enough for now. I am tentatively planning to take the train (if I can travel) to visit some relatives in Washington and drop in on you and Martha this Spring – say April or May – and perhaps we can continue. I'd like to hear about your days as a POW and I'll trade you my experiences as a casualty. Then I will go to visit relatives in Boston and continue North.

I've included some things you may not need on the off chance that there are some names that ring a bell. I may find some more items as I get ready to move to SF and I will send them on to you. (I'm a great filer but a lousy retriever.)

Best to you and Martha and your ever-growing clan!!!!

Hal

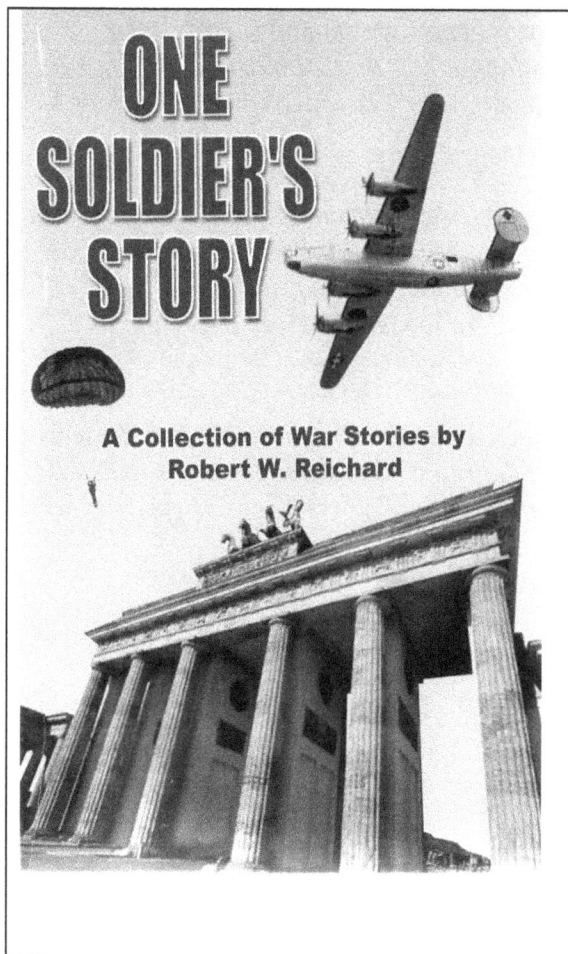

Below is an excerpt from Robert W. Reichard's book:

One Soldier's Story

Mr. Reichard served as a bombardier on a B-24 Liberator in the **456th Bomb Group, 745th Squadron** from October 1944 until the end of the war in May 1945. He flew 25 missions over Nazi held Europe.

One Soldier's Story
by Robert W. Reichard
ISBN# 1-932205-80-2

Word Association Publishers
205 5th Avenue
Tarentum, PA 15084

http://www.amazon.com

745th Bomb Squadron

(Excerpted from *One Soldier's Story*)

We were located near Cerignola, Italy, close to Stornara. It was a farming area. The 456th Bomb Group (H) was located on a knoll at the SW corner of the airstrip. The airstrip was laid out in a north/south direction. The airstrip was one of the eight satellite airstrips around Foggia, which had been utilized by the Luftwaffe before they were chased out. Foggia was to our north. The squadrons were located around the perimeter of the airstrip. There was the 744th at the SW corner, the 745th at the NW corner, and the 746th and 747th were on the east side. Our ground contacts with each other were nil except for briefings and the resulting combat missions.

The Runway at Stornara
Courtesy of *456th Bomb Group Association*

We were dispersed in an olive orchard and lived in tents. In fact, upon our arrival, the four officers, were given a pyramidal tent to erect. In time we would move into a tent, which had been upgraded, by a crew who had completed their missions and were on their way home. The upgraded tents had tile floors, stove, shower, and the walls were extended. Everything had been scrounged. The shower stall occupied one corner of the tent and was fed water by a fighter plane drop tank, which had been elevated above the shower head level. A make shift stove heated the water by using aviation gasoline. The main tent heater was a 55 gallon drum which had been cut in half and inverted over a fireproof base. 100 octane gas was allowed to flow in, through metal tubing, from an outside drum and this wound up in an improvised burner. The burner was a metal can filled with sand which had been placed inside the overturned drum. The gas was allowed to drip into the sand after a burning piece of paper was placed in it from a hole in the side of the drum. The chimney was made of empty 88mm casings which had been fired by the German anti-aircraft, when they had been in the area. The tent area was enlarged by untying the side walls, building a wall around tent, big enough to accept the tent sides when they were moved from a vertical to horizontal position. That increased the tent floor space outward the length of the tent wall. The tile floors and walls were usually done by hiring Italian help.

Lighting the tent stove could be hazardous to your health as the navigator learned. He didn't put the lighted paper in the burner first. He turned on the fuel, walked around the stove, struck a match, I yelled, "Stop" too late and he put the match into the stove opening. The result was a loud explosion and a trip to the medics to treat his badly burned arm. The air to gas combustion was bad and that resulted in clogged chimneys. This was overcome by beating on the chimney while the stove was on. The chimney spewed forth burning pieces of carbon which burned holes through the tent tops. As a result it was not unusual to lie in bed at night and be able to study the stars without going outside.

We ate in the mess hall which was a make shift affair of canvas, masonry, and wood. It also served as the squadron officers' club in the evening. The food was of the canned and dried variety and the eggs were dehydrated. (On our missions we carried "K" rations, which were composed of 3 different types: breakfast with canned scrambled eggs, dinner with a can of cheese or canned dog food. These were eaten cold and you had crackers in place of bread. There was a packet containing 5 cigarettes, toilet paper, and other goodies.) At meal time we would have a long wait, so we would play "Hearts" (simple card game) while we waited to be fed. In the evenings we gathered in the club to put our worries aside. It was pot luck as to what you were going to drink, but as long as it contained alcohol it filled the bill. The only mix available for mixed drinks was grapefruit juice aplenty. I hated it and to this day it is not my cup-of-tea. There was a piano and at least one of the officers could play it. When he started playing a group would get together, and oh how they would harmonize. A favorite was "Three Jolly Coachman". I couldn't carry a tune, but I would get in my cups and would join in. The result was amazing -- they would stop singing and stare at me. I would take the hint and go back to my cup.

Our latrine facilities were the many holed outhouse or pipes that had been shoved in the ground, throughout the tent area, so you would urinate in designated places instead of everywhere. (I don't know how the modern army will handle that one with female troopers.) I guess that confined the smell to selected spots. Foxholes were everywhere, but there were too many injuries as a result of falling into them as we left the Club to get to our tents. They were filled in to cut the casualty rate. The tent ropes still took their toll and they couldn't be removed without doing away with our shelter. We had to learn to navigate better.

There was electricity in the evenings, so we were allowed to tap in and put a light bulb in our tent. In the daytime the generators supplied the orderly room, medics, operations, and supply room. I found that electric line draping through an olive tree along side our tent and tapped it. We could now enjoy those dreary fall days writing letters in our tent. That worked fine, but one day we were cleaning outside the tent and one of the party had a machete. And what does one do with a machete in hand if there is a tree nearby? Right, he swings at the trunk for the hell of it. Only this swing was different. It produced sparks much to his amazement, so what to do? Swing again to recreate the phenomenon. He did and there was another display of sparks and our daytime electric power was cut. He had severed the power line tap where it ran down the trunk of the olive tree and into the tent.

There was an Armed Forces Radio Station (AFRS) at Foggia, but radios were few and far between. A select few had recovered some from crashes and put them on line. One tent had a novel setup. They had the ingenuity to stick a wire antenna out the top of their tent and this they connected to a combination of earphone, wire coil, and a razor blade. The result was a unpowered crystal radio which brought in the AFRS Radio Station. The end of the coiled wire had been bent to touch the razor blade and that acted like a crystal.

The main duty was to fly combat missions. When we weren't doing that we were training in the air or on the ground, or pulling different duty officer assignments, which included censoring mail, and MP duty in Orta Nova. They even brought a bombardier training platform which we ran in one of the group buildings. I was glad when I used the last one in Bombardier School, but here it was again. I trained as a radar operator, but never flew a combat sortie as one.

When we arrived at our squadron we were told that our tour would be completed when we had flown 50 combat missions. Missions above a certain parallel of latitude were credited as 2 missions. When I started flying, the targets were all 2 for 1 and I would be going home after 25 times out. That soon ended, and our missions were called sorties and it was 1 for 1 wherever you went and the magic number was 35. Briefings were held in the early morning hours before each raid. They were held at Group Headquarters. A general briefing and the specialized briefings for pilots, navigators, bombardiers, etc. after.

When we returned from the sortie we were interrogated at Group Headquarters, but we picked up a donut and a container of coffee from the Red Cross girls before entering the interrogation building. The girls were great, but they must have been selected because of their homely looks, so the war effort wouldn't be affected. (However our radar training officer dated one and we nicknamed him "Radar" because like radar, he would pick anything up.) At this time we had our chance to report any future targets which we had seen, such as railway traffic build-ups, the number of chutes exiting a disabled bomber, target results, anti-aircraft, Luftwaffe intervention, etc. Back in the squadron the medics issued a 2 ounce shot of American whiskey. It was for medical purposes and they accounted for each 2 ounce by your pay roll signature.

Church services were held at Group Headquarters. I had developed a strong sense of religion along the way. As an aviation cadet I received a copy of the 91st Psalm and a picture of Christ from a woman in Lehighton, Pa, by the name of Hawk. I think she was the wife of anther cadet who entered the service with me. He became a pilot. I kept them with me and they were my crutch. I read the Psalm nightly and carried it with me always. It was my talisman. I didn't ask God for any favors except, if I had to be hit, do it right, as I didn't want to lie bleeding, in the cold, without aid for the 2 to 4 hours the return trip usually took.

For more great stories by **Robert W. Reichard** *about flying in B-24 Liberators during World War II, serving with the ground troops in the Korean War, being posted in Berlin during the Cold War, and much more, order --* **One Soldier's Story** *-- at* http://www.amazon.com.

Author's Notes and References

This book would not have been possible without the help of the following:

Howard N. Hartman and **Edward L. DeMent** who provided eye witness accounts of the April 3, 1944 mission and their experiences inside German POW camps.

Michael J. Dancisak, Ph.D at Tulane University who graciously provided many of the photographs for the book.

Hans Halberstadt (http://www.militaryphoto.com) who also graciously sent photographs and letters from his father's collection.

Robert R. Perry for providing information on missions flown after April 3, 1944.

Robert W. Reichard, author of *One Soldier's Story*, available at http://www.amazon.com, who found me and gave me the keys to unlock the mystery of my father's crew.

Fred H. Riley, the 456th Bomb Group Historian who provided the crew list of the *Boojum* and contact information for the surviving crewmen.

Roy Firestone, the webmaster of the 456th Bomb Group Association web site, http://www.456thbombgroup.org, who provided several photos from the web site.

Robert S. Capps, whose book *Flying Colt* (available at http://www.authorhouse.com) provided great detail about the 456th Bomb Group's missions in early 1944.

United States Air Force Academy Libraries, http://www.usafa.af.mil/df/dflib, for photographs of Stalag Luft III and Stalag Luft VIIa.

Frances A. Abner, my mother, for digging through the attic and finding my father's service records.

Ellen M. Abner, my loving wife, for proofreading and editing the second edition.

Last but not least, I have to thank my father, **Frederick G. Abner, Jr.** whose remembrance lives on forever, and whose inspiration - even from beyond – flows throughout the pages of this work.

David F. Abner